POETS' HOMES

Henry W. Longfellow

POETS' HOMES.

PEN AND PENCIL SKETCHES

OF

AMERICAN POETS AND THEIR HOMES.

BY

R. H. STODDARD AND OTHERS.

BOSTON:

D. LOTHROP AND COMPANY,

FRANKLIN ST., CORNER OF HAWLEY.

James B Hedge, Sr

Recat. 11-20-46 frn

CONTENTS.

2107

CONTENTS.

HENRY WADSWORTH LONGFELLOW.

IF it may be said of any living man that he is known
all over the world, it may be said of Henry Wads-
worth Longfellow.   His words seem to travel on the
swift rays of light that penetrate unto the uttermost
parts of the earth.   James T. Fields, in his Longfellow
lecture, tells of the strange and far-away places in
which he has felt his heart warmed at sight of a well-
worn copy of Longfellow's poems.   He has the touch
of nature that makes the whole world kin, for he is
not more warmly appreciated in his native land than
in the hearts and homes on the other side of the
world.

Everyone knows the brief outlines of the poet's life.
He was born in Portland, Maine, in 1807.   He entered Bowdoin College when he was fourteen years
old, and graduated there in 1825.   He traveled in
Europe three or four years, preparing himself for the

professorship of modern languages in his own college. In 1835 he was elected Professor of Modern Languages and Belles-Lettres in Harvard College. He held this position until 1854, when he resigned. He has since lived in Cambridge, in the old Craigie House on Brattle street. His literary life began very early. While an undergraduate he published many of his most beautiful poems in different newspapers. It may cheer discouraged young writers to know that for one of these, "Sandalphon," he received as payment a year's subscription to the newspaper in which it was published. In recalling this, he said laughingly that it was not so bad as the fortune of a friend of his, who, after having contributed largely to a certain paper, was invited by the genial editor to take an ice, by way of making things square between them. Can it be that our magnificent editors of to-day have descended from such untoward sires?

Longfellow's first book was published by the Harpers. He sold the copyright for five hundred dollars and thought himself fortunate. Doubtless his publishers were as well satisfied. From that time his literary career has been one unvarying success.

As regards that other life, dearer than his public labors, more sacred than his intellectual record, — here, too, Longfellow has been written Blessed.

True, he has known poignant sorrow. Death has entered his home and taken from it his dearest. That this is a sorrow ever-abiding, and one from which in one sense he will never recover, the years have proved. His melancholy is but dimly seen, like a smoke curling upward from a blazing fire, yet it is present always, veiling his cheerfulness and saddening his smiles. " I never heard him make but one allusion to the great grief of his life," said an intimate friend. " We were speaking of Schiller's fine poem, 'The Ring of Polycrates,' and he said, ' It was just so with me, I was too happy. I might fancy the gods envied me — if I could fancy heathen gods.' "

As if striving to make amends, fate has given him every other good gift ; fortune, fame, and the sweeter gifts of love, gratitude and reverence from those he has cheered, helped and elevated ; a lovely family whose youth and brightness shed sunshine over his evening days, and a home that must be a joy forever to the poet's soul.

. . . .

Perhaps I could not interest any readers better than in telling them something about this beautiful home. It was rich in associations when Longfellow first came to it as a lodger. It was builded midway in the last century, by a gentleman of family and distinction, Col. John Vassol, whose gravestone in Cambridge bears upon it a sculptured goblet and a sun. After the Revolutionary War the house was bought by one Thomas Tracy, who appears to have been a sort of American Vathek, emulating, as far as possible in an uncongenial clime, the magnificent doings of the Eastern prince. Traditions float down to us of the lavish opulence of these, the golden days of Vassol Hall; how wine flowed like water, servants lived like kings, a hundred guests sat down every day at the banquet table, and from the far-off lands of the Orient, treasures of silk and jewels and gold flowed into the coffers of the lucky Thomas Tracy. But debts grew many and friends grew few. The generous host found himself one day bankrupt; his career cut short; for, unlike our modern princes he did not fail — to get rich.

With the passing of his wealth, clouds gathered about the old home. We hear of it no more until it came into the hands of the last owner save one — Andrew Craigie. It proved a white elephant on his hands, as it had on those of his predecessors. The expenses it entailed ruined him; necessity obliged him to part with all save eight of the two hundred acres originally included in the estate, and after his death Mrs. Craigie was forced to let lodgings to the youth of Harvard — pigmies all to her, though to us such intellectual giants as Everett, Worcester, Sparks and Longfellow were among them.

Of this old reduced gentlewoman some curious stories are told. She was tall and stately, of a dignity that commanded deference, and a sternness that forbade love. Even her husband stood in awe of his august spouse. We have more than one ghastly picture of her as she appears in the reminiscences of those who knew her in her age and loneliness and pride.

On one occasion her young poet-lodger, entering her parlor in the morning, found her sitting by the open window, through which innumerable canker-worms had crawled from the trees that they were devouring outside. They had fastened themselves to her dress, and hung in little writhing festoons from the white turban on her head. Her visitor, surprised and shocked, asked if she would do nothing to destroy the worms. Raising her eyes from her book — she sat calmly reading, like indifference on a monument — she said, in tones of solemn rebuke: "Young man, have not our fellow-worms as good a right to live as we?" an answer which throws Uncle Tobey's "Go, little fly!" quite into the shade.

As this grim old lady lay a-dying she sent for the

lodger to bid him farewell.   He approached the bed-side and looked silently upon the spectral figure, the withered face, the gray hair.   Suddenly drawing the bed-clothes close around her, she opened her keen sunken eyes, bright one moment before dimming with death, and uttered this strange greeting and farewell :

"Young man, never marry, for see how ugly an old woman looks in bed!"

In 1843 the house was bought by Mr. Longfellow, and from that time, with tender love and reverent care he has adorned, beautified and perfected it.   He has made it what it had not been in all its changing fortunes — a home.   Taste has guided the hand of wealth, and from year to year have been added beau-ties of art, curiosities from every land, and sacred relics.

The very atmosphere is different from that of other houses.   It has a sacred hush, due in part, it may be, to the all-subduing power of association —

> "Once, ah, once within these walls
> One whom memory oft recalls, —
> The Father of his Country dwelt —"

yet none the less a result of that nameless influence — intangible and fragrant as the odor of a flower —

that emanates from pure and beautiful minds, and makes the spiritual life of a home.

The house is set back from the road, behind a lilac hedge blossoming in spring with purple and white. On either side are broad verandahs from which one can look across to Charles River and the blue hills of Milton.

The meadow between is always bathed in sunshine, and on its green slope some new picture is ever forming itself; children at play, mild-faced cows cropping the grass, or the little woman in the red cloak, whom artists delight in, as the needed bit of color in a landscape.

October is the best month for seeing the place in all its beauty. Then the clustering lilacs, still green with summer freshness, are over-run with the wild, red beauty of riotous woodbine, dying in a glow of defiance. Then from the trees fluttering leaves of welcome float into the outstretched hand, or fall gently before the advancing feet.

The old elm at the door is stripped of its leaves, and you wonder at the fine network of interlacing boughs. Charles River, now clearly seen, winds along like an S of running silver. October, too, is the time to walk in the old-fashioned garden — a garden such as Andrew Marvell's must have been.

> " I have a garden of my own,
> But so with roses overgrown,
> And lilies, that you would it guess
> To be a little wilderness."

This " little wilderness " is shut out from inhar-
monious sights and sounds.   To come from the
noisy world into its cool retreat, is from Avernus to
the Happy Valley.

One can imagine fairies in the flower-cups, and
spirits gliding down the shaded walks.   Spirits of
stately dames in embroidered petticoats and high-
heeled slippers, and gallant courtiers with sheathed
swords and powdered queues; and with these
majestic ghosts, the fair young muse of poetry,
gazing at them with clear eyes unabashed, knowing that at her hands they lose not one grace or
remembered glory.

Sitting in the half-ruined summer-house, I almost
wished the doctrine of Pythagoras were reversed,
and that my soul might pass into the flower growing beside me, or the bird singing overhead.   I
envied the little golden lady-bugs that sunned
their magnificence in the poet's garden, and wondered if the lazy caterpillars knew what good
fortune awaited them as butterflies in this earthly
paradise.

Perhaps the most interesting room in the house

is Longfellow's study. Here most of the poet's hours are spent, the quiet only broken by the chimes of the old clock in the corner. It is one of those antique time-pieces, higher than a man's head, with a round moon face at the top, such as are found in some old New England houses, and are a sufficient guarantee for the respectability of the family. An open fire burns cheerily in the grate.

An orange-tree stands in the window, and near it an Egyptian stork keeps watch. A table in the centre of the room is heaped with books and papers, and has a look of orderly disorder. Its choicest treasure is Coleridge's inkstand. Here, too, is an early volume of Coleridge's poems, annotated in his own handwriting, which is as scraggly as that of a genius ought to be. On this table are piles of unanswered letters ; only a sharp-toothed mouse could get through them in a month's time.

That which future generations will regard with most interest in this room, is a book-case filled with Longfellow's own works in the original manuscripts. They are handsomely bound, as befits the clear, beautiful writing, and make a noble collection.

It is a pity to divide them, yet what one should monopolize such a heritage? Perhaps public gift will eventually be made of them. Some baby now unborn may donate them where they will be safe through the generations.

Among the pictures here are crayon likenesses of Emerson, Sumner and Hawthorne, all taken when these famous men were in the flush of youth.

Passing through the hall we enter "Lady Washington's Drawing Room." The furniture is white satin covered with gay flowers in vines and clusters; arm-chairs and sofas are heaped with soft cushions covered with the same material. The carpet is a bed of flowers.

The effect is greatly heightened by a large mirror opening another gay vista, and a picture in gorgeous colors extending from wall to ceiling. It is one of Copley's, "The Grandchildren of Sir William Pepprell." A quaint little maiden, in a high cap and stiff bodice, a youth with flowing curls, and a wooden-looking poodle compose the group. The picture is set in a massive burnished frame, and the effect would be oppressive in another room, but is in admirable harmony with this state apartment.

On an *etageré* laden with treasures is an agate cup from the hand of no less a master, Benvenuto Cellini — clear, exquisitely carved, graceful in shape, and guarded by two tiny, open-mouthed dragons. It was sent to him from the collection of the poet Rogers, and has therefore a double value in Longfellow's eyes. As he holds it in his hand and points out its beauties, one can but think what a crowd of associations are gathering in its delicate cup.

In the dining-room we see rare old china, a modern picture of a cardinal in red, walking in the Borghese gardens, and several family portraits. Among them is Buchanan Read's picture of "Longfellow's daughters," that has been photographed so often, the "blue-eyed banditti" that the poet father has so charmingly apostrophized in "The Children's Hour:"

> "Grave Alice and laughing Allegra,
>   And Edith with golden hair."

From this room we pass into a long, narrow hall, running the length of the house. At its head great Jove looks before him with big, unseeing eyes, while on either side are those lovely marble women, who, in spite of Lord Byron's couplet, —

> " I've seen more beauty, ripe and real,
>   Than all the nonsense of their stone ideal,"

still hold their own — as embodied ideas in human shape — against their living sisters.

The library is the most beautiful room in the house; dark and rich in tone, with a look of spacious elegance and home-like comfort. On three sides the walls are lined with books. The bronzes and Japanese screens are studies.

Here hangs a portrait of Liszt. The back-ground is dark, and he is dressed in the long black convent robe. High above his head he holds a lighted candle. The rays shape themselves like a halo round his head, and throw into fine relief the thin, spirited face.

Mr. Longfellow saw him thus for the first time as he stood in the convent door, peering out into the night. The vision impressed itself on the poet, and he persuaded Liszt to have his picture painted.

From the library a passage leads to the billiard-room, now fallen into disuse, and converted into an æsthetic lumber-room, where one would delight to dream away a rainy day.

The rooms up-stairs are as full of interest as those below.

One suite has been fitted up by Mr. Longfellow's son in Japanese style. The wall-paper is of neutral tint, ornamented with Japanese fans in groups of twos and threes. The heathen gods frown at you, national arms are collected, tables are heaped with Japanese books made on the principal of cat stairs, and photographs of Japanese beauties, with button-hole mouths, and long, bright eyes, abound.

This article would become a catalogue of description should I try to enumerate half the curiosities to be seen in this grand old house. One cabinet alone, with its medley of treasures, is worth an afternoon's study. Here is a bit of Dante's coffin ; there an agate cylinder, and some brilliant African beetles. Two canes attract you ; one is made from the spar of the ship on which the Star Spangled Banner was written, the other comes from Acadie, and is surmounted by a hideous head, which, Mr. Longfellow says, with a twinkle in his eye, was the poet's idea of Evangeline.

Your readers are probably all familiar with Saxe Holm's exquisite story, "Esther Wynn's Love Letters," and will recall how Uncle Jo found these letters on the cellar-stairs ; how mysterious terrors

gathered round them until it was discovered that
they slipped through a crack in the upper stairs
where they had been nailed for safe keeping.
This is a true incident. It was Mr. Longfellow's
house that held the letters, and he who found
them on the cellar-stairs.

They were written to the husband of the old
lady who sat with her fellow-worms in the parlor — and were placed by him in their hiding-place
— for what reason none will ever know. They
were not such love-letters as Esther Wynn's, but
an interest scarcely less tragic attached to them.
Mr. Longfellow had intended making them a subject
for a poem ; but Saxe Holm forestalled him in her
story.

.   .   .   .

Longfellow is now nearly seventy years of age.
He is of medium height, well made, with no sign
of age in figure or walk. His head and face are
eminently poetic. His forehead is broad, benig-
nant, and full. The great charm of his face centres
in his eyes ; of an unclouded blue, deep-set, under
overhanging brows, they hold an indescribable expression of thought and tenderness. Though seamed
with many wrinkles, his face is rarely without the
rosy hue of health, and would appear that of a

much younger man but for its frame of snow-white hair. Hair and whiskers are long, abundant and wavy, and give the poet the look of a patriarch.

His manner has a child's simplicity, yet is of an impregnable dignity. Tolerant to all opinions, courteous to all men, he is approached nearly only by the few. When with friends there is a dash of gentle humor in his talk, more mirth-provoking than livelier sallies from wittier men.

In his home his hospitality is proverbial. Bret Harte has called him the ideal poet, and he is ideal host as well. His gentle tact and exquisite courtesy remind one of that fine compliment paid to Villemand — which is a fine definition of politeness — "when he spoke to a lady one would think he had offered her a boquet."

Nothing can ruffle his courtesy ; not even such remarks as were once made to him by some English visitors, neither nice nor wise — that "there were no ruins in this country, so they thought they would call and see him."

He is emphatically the poet of the beautiful, and his life is as rounded and complete as one of his own sonnets or a Beethoven symphony. He is not one of those great men who must be seen, like an oil-painting, at a distance, but the nearer one ap-

proaches, the finer show the outlines and shadings
of his character.   Success has not made him indifferent to the aspirations of the unknown.   The young
poet who goes to Longfellow with his verses need not
fear a cold reception nor an indifferent listener.
Sympathy he will surely find; and should his verses
contain one glimmer of the sacred fire, that encour-
agement for want of which many a young genius
has been stifled.

He is still an earnest worker, composing with
great care.   Time has taken from him only the gold
of his hair and the smoothness of his brow, and has
given him year by year added grace and sweetness
and strength.   Wide-spread as his influence has
been, yet his mission has hardly begun; for as
long as the heart of humanity shall beat, his voice
will be heard in tones of music, singing words of
consolation and hope.

MR. LONGFELLOW'S HOME, CAMBRIDGE, MASS.

JOHN G. WHITTIER.

THE old county of Essex, Massachusetts, is fertile in suggestions of poetry. It is dotted with sunny villages, shady farms, landscapes diversified with pure, clear rivers, and land-slopes before which rolls the broad, open sea. Every old farm-house has a legend, and every town its quaint bit of colonial history.

The Merrimac, that industrious river, goes dimpling through it to the sea, shaded in summer by wooded hills, and reflecting in autumn the leafy rubies of newly-cut timber-lands, or the grand forms of old trees.

"Beautiful! beautiful!" exclaimed President Washington, in his journey to Haverhill in 1789, as his eye fell on the sparkling waters of the Merrimac. "Haverhill is the pleasantest village I ever passed through!"

In this pleasant old New England town there was born, in 1808, a poet, with whose ballads, we doubt not, most of our readers are acquainted. He is a descendant of an old Quaker family, which settled along the banks of the Merrimac when Haverhill was a frontier settlement, and the Indians burned its houses, and carried unhappy Hannah Dunstan into a long captivity.

The Colonial Whittiers, refusing the protection of the garrison in these perilous times, relied upon just and kind treatment of the Indians for defence. They found their peace principles and their habit of dealing justly with all men a more sure defence than muskets or stockades. The family used to hear the Indians at the windows on the still winter nights, and occasionally would see a red face and fierce eyes at the window-pane. But though their neighbors were murdered and their property destroyed, the Quakers were never molested.

The poet's early home was an ample old farm-house in East Haverhill. As you may read about it in "Snow Bound" it need not be described here. In recent years it has fallen somewhat into decay, though its grand old trees and primitive expression have been partially preserved.

The poet, when quite young, was sent to school to

a queer old pedagogue, who received pupils in a room in his own house. The teacher did not succeed in governing his wife, however well he may have gov-

J. G. WHITTIER.

erned his scholars. Like Oliver Goldsmith, who gave his pupils gingerbread and told them stories, this easy-going man adopted the persuasive method of preserving order and imparting instruction.

" Through the cracked and crazy wall
Came the cradle-rock and squall,
And the goodman's voice at strife
With his shrill and tipsy wife,
Luring us by stories old,
With a comic unction told,
More than by the eloquence
Of terse birchen arguments."

— The young scholar had few books of poetry in his early years, but nature was to him a continual poem. The warm grasp of friendship, the blue sky of spring, and the changing splendors of fall, — these were to him sources of poetic inspiration. He was a mere boy when he began to express the glowing feelings of his soul in verse.

One day he ventured to send a poem, which he had copied in blue ink on some coarse paper, to an anti-slavery journal called the *Free Press*, published in Newburyport. The editor of the paper, William Lloyd Garrison, found the poem on the floor of his office, it having been tucked under the door by the postman. His first impulse was to throw the manuscript into the waste-basket ; but being a conscientious man he gave it a reading. He had not read far before he discovered in the lines evidence that they were written by a true poet.

The poem appeared in the *Free Press*. Other poems

from the same writer came to the office, and they impressed Mr. Garrison so favorably that he made inquiries of the postman whence they came. He was told that they probably had been sent by a farmer's son in East Haverhill.

Mr. Garrison thinking that he ought to encourage so promising a writer, rode over to East Haverhill to call on his new contributor. He found him at work with his father on the farm. The young man acknowledged the authorship of the poems. The visit of the editor must have been a happy surprise to him, for appreciation is never more stimulating than in youth.

Mr. Whittier — for such our readers will have recognized to be the poet's name — began life as a teacher. He came to Boston when about twenty-one years of age, where he was employed editorially on the *New England Weekly*. Returning to Haverhill he was elected to the Massachusetts Legislature, and afterwards went to Philadelphia as editor of the *Freeman*. But his love of a quiet life led him again to the Merrimac, and he settled in the rural town of Amesbury, where the moral, political and pastoral poems, by which he is best known to the world, were mostly written.

His home is a plain, neat house, in the most quiet part of the town. At a little distance the open coun-

try stretches in front of its windows.   Near it stands
a Quaker meeting-house, on the border of a grove of
birch and pine, around which a shady road goes wind-

HOME OF J. G. WHITTIER.

ing through the light, sandy soil.   Not far behind it
rolls the Merrimac through hill-slopes variegated with

glossy birches, billowy oaks, and dark clusters of laurels and pines.

The poet's home was, for many years, in charge of his maiden sister, Elizabeth H. Whittier, a woman of lovely character, who fully sympathized with her brother in his literary work. It is said that he was accustomed to submit to her criticism the first copies of whatever he wrote. The old Quaker preachers, anti-slavery reformers, and many eminent writers, used to visit the Whittiers at this time, and enjoy the cosy hospitality of the sunny rooms. A well-tilled garden blossomed without, household pets added to the charming simplicity within, and the wooded hills, which enclosed the homestead like a park, rolled away in the distance to the busy river that ran to the sea.

The associations of Whittier's poetry are almost everywhere to be found in the county in which he lives. The Merrimac, which clasps many historic towns in its arm, on its bending way to the sea, is his river of song.

Marblehead, perhaps the quaintest town in America, with its sea-worn rocks, and its light-houses flaming at evening above the silvery lagoons of the ocean, is the scene of Skipper Ireson's punishment. New-

buryport, where Whitefield's coffin may still be
seen, —

> " Under the church on Federal Street,"

is the scene of " The Preacher."

The curving beaches that sweep away from the old
coast towns of Gloucester, Ipswich and Marblehead,
are accurately described in "The Tent on the Beach,"
and in other poems. "The Shoemakers," "The
Huskers," "The Drovers," and "The Fishermen,"
are subjects of poems that but picture familiar scenes
in Amesbury and in the neighboring towns.

Most of his historical ballads are associated with
places which the old inhabitants point out to the
stranger who visits Essex County, and the incidents
of many of them were told at the farmer's firesides
a hundred years ago. Like the brothers Grimm in
Germany, the poet has collected these old tales, and
given them enduring fame by clothing them in the
choicest language.

Mr. Whittier wears the silver crown of seventy
years. His poems are among the æsthetic treasures
of every intelligent family, as far as the English language is spoken. They are recited in every school
and quoted from many a platform and pulpit. Their
influences range widely, and always for good.

2107

It is indeed a blessed life that multiplies such influences among mankind! "His poetry," says one of his old friends, "bursts from the heart with the fire and energy of the ancient prophet, but his noble simplicity of character is the delight of us all!"

MRS. A. D. T. WHITNEY.

ALSTEAD, N. H., Sept., 1875.

M^Y DEAR EDITH: I cannot let the pleasant
summer pass quite away with St. Michael,
who "keeps the gate ablaze with autumn's heraldry,"
without giving you a sketch of our life "among the
hills," here at Mrs. Whitney's summer home, in the old
farm-house on Alstead heights. You, and the "other
girls," will like to hear something about our fashion
of living in this primitive part of the world, I'm sure;
but you would enjoy the being here a great deal
more; for, to my mind, it is about the perfection of a
simple, unfettered, charming country life; and Alstead
belongs to one of the loveliest regions of picturesque.
New England.

Mrs. Whitney's very own home is in Milton, near
Boston, you remember; but she has not lived there
for several years, not since before she went abroad,
while Alstead has been her abiding-place during three

or four summers, and was last winter as well. This
season she has filled the house with a " picked " party
of her friends, nearly all Boston people — Hubites, all
of whom, in their own manner of speech, I " admire "
to know. As our landlady says, we are eight "per-
manents ; " but there are several " temperies," in the
language of " Emery Ann," who have made the agreeable variety in our household. This doesn't include
the farmer's family of four, the smart Yankee help,
and the great brindle cat, the handsomest and most
dignified of his race, whom his mistress endearingly
addresses as " Tommy " and " my child," but who is
known to the rest of us as " Lord Bacon." I wish
you could appreciate the *tonsorial* twang with which
the name is enunciated. Mr. Whitney, who has a
tender heart for " Our Dumb Animals," is addicted
to feeding him surreptitiously at table ; but " Lord
Bacon's " mother doesn't approve, and orders him
peremptorily into the kitchen when she sees him
yielding to the temptation of proffered cheese and
tidbits.

We have delightful times in one way and another
Mrs. Whitney is, in a manner, the center around which
all revolve. Her room is the nucleus of the house ;
she presides at the table, and she is deferred to naturally by each one of us. We depend entirely upon our

own resources for amusement, since we are in true seclusion, in the "deep, green country," Alstead being off the line of ordinary summer travel.

It is seventeen miles from Keene, and six or eight from Bellows Falls; and a lumbering, big, antique stage travels every afternoon from "The Falls" to Alstead, carrying mail and passengers, with a curiosity in the shape of an octogenarian driver, as hale and active as another man of fifty.

We leave the pretty white village, with its roofs and spires nestling amid the trees and embosomed among the hills, and "wind about, and in, and out" at the base of them until we begin an ascent two miles up a three-mile hill that rises steeply to the table-land where the Town Center is built; and we reach our old-fashioned farm-house, which has stood here over a hundred years, with its barns opposite, screened by two stately, wide-spreading elms, and the huge old poplar on the piazza side. I have often wondered what old Puritan with an artist's eye it could have been who selected a building site of such unrivaled beauty, commanding so glorious a sweep of country, bounded by those mountain ranges, in "purple distance fair."

One croquet ground is in the green door yard at the front, and this is Mrs. Whitney's special domain, for she is an enthusiastic and skillful player. There is another on the slope to the left below the piazza, frequented by the less aspiring croqueters, who say, jocosely, that they haven't graduated into the scientific ring yet. You need not ask me where I belong! Well, the view is much finer from our ground, at any rate; and I solace myself with the beauty of the hills and the splendor of the sunsets, when I make particularly unlucky hits. You would enjoy a game with Mrs. Whitney. She would be an opponent worthy of your mallet, for she handles hers like the mistress of the situation, even when she plays with Ben and Doris, who are renowned champions.

This is the pleasantest spot in all Alstead — the "Place of Beautiful Streams." (One of us discovered the Saxon meaning of the name in some old book, the other day.) I wish I could send you a pencil-sketch which would do justice to the place.

The beautiful fields fall and swell away from us in lovely curve and undulation, rich with many shades of green and gold. The near hills darkly wooded with birch and pine, the distant mountains, in all their varying, exquisite tints of blues and grays and purples, make the gift of sight a perpetual joy.

Over the little latticed entrance porch, where we often gather after breakfast to enjoy the sparkling

freshness of the morning and chat for a few minutes
on the sunny stoop, a luxuriant vine is trained, spread-
ing and climbing up the sides of the house. Our
hostess calls the flowers "Morning Beauties;" and
the vine curtains greenly one window of Mrs. Whitney's room. She is very fond of the delicate bell-like
flowers, with their green heart-shaped leaves, and
gathers some every morning to fill her little vases
and dishes, for the decoration of her tables and mantel-shelf.

Beside the bower-window stands her desk, near the
well-filled bookcase. Don't you think you would like
to sit down at Mrs. Whitney's own desk and write
your letters, as I have done? There's quite an inspiration in it. There are pictures on the walls, but the
one you would like best is an exquisite, full-sized engraving of a painting which Mrs. Whitney loves very
much, and which a dear friend sent her last Christmas, — the "Mother and Child" of the Holbein in
the Dresden Gallery. Then, there are some bright
autumn leaves painted by her "own girl," which an
old countryman who came up here to do some work
the other day took for real, saying "he'd some to
home could beat them for color." Mrs. Whitney herself paints, and is filling a large book with lovely
vines and wild flowers and colored branches from the

woods, done in water colors; and she brought home some exquisite little copies in water-color of pictures abroad. I should like to show you a tender Madonna face, from Raphael, which I covet, and one of Fra Angelico's rainbow-winged angels.

Sometimes several of us sit and sew and talk in this pleasant, shaded room, or "spill over," as she would say, into the hall and porch, or on the stairway. This is a very sociable fashion we have; and we keep all our doors open, except when we are busy working or studying. But we oftenest congregate on the cool piazza, where Mrs. Whitney has her reclining chair and camp chairs carried out for our greater comfort, and where she sometimes reads to us while we work.

We have particularly jolly times at dinner, when we have been apart during the morning, some of us wandering in the woods, others busy in our own rooms. By way of variety we often make French our table-talk, and we find French jokes infinitely amusing. Mrs. Whitney is especially charming at table with her *air gracieux*, in her dainty bit of a white lace cap, and the white crocheted shawl thrown over her light cambric dress. None of us profess to make grand toilets at Alstead; but some people have the knack of making themselves bewitching under whatever circumstances.

3

Opposite Mrs. Whitney sits her husband, a fine-looking, gray-haired gentleman, with a delightfully benevolent face. Besides being a friend of cats, he is a great walker, the chief of our pedestrian excursions, and indefatigable in all he undertakes.

We have done a good deal of driving about the country this summer. Fancy a wagon load of us starting out for a long morning's ride, or a day's excursion. You know how merry such parties are. We have adorned our new whip with red, white, and blue streamers, and trot gayly up and down hill and through the village streets, with our patriotic ensign flying on the breeze.

We are generally drawn by two remarkable steeds, which some wicked wags among us have christened "Hydrophobia" and "The Caterpillar," because one of them seems to abhor water, as Nature was once said to abhor a vacuum, and the other drags his leisurely length along, up hill and down, with a sublime scorn of whip or cheering word.

One charming excursion we made was to Keene, and we were gone the livelong day, driving up hill and down dale, with constant shifting mountain views, grand old Monadnock and Ascutney ever and anon looming up our horizon like some rugged monarch with his royal consort. On our return from the pleas-

ant New England town, through the pretty valley of
the Ashuelot, we were caught in a heavy rain storm,
but defied the elements with umbrellas and water-
proofs in spite of our open wagon, and when the sun
shone out presently through the still falling shower,
a perfect and exquisite rainbow was flung against the
green mountain slope to our right, each soft and brilliant hue in the arch of color defined against the vivid
emerald.

Mrs. Whitney says such rainbows cast on the earth,
as it were, are not unusual in mountain regions ; but
I had never seen one before.

I wish I could take you into Alstead woods with
us, my dear. I'm inclined to believe there are few
more fascinating pursuits than the following up of the
beds of the mountain brooks, which abound here.
The ferns and mosses are beyond anything I ever
dreamed of. There are endless delicate varieties in
the damp, shady places ; and graceful great clumps
and clusters of ferns spring up everywhere. Of course
we have pressed ferns by the hundreds, and made
ferneries, and gone into birch-bark work.

There is a grove about three miles from here, where
one actually *wades* in an acre of maidenhair, not to
mention other places where it abounds. I never before found it excepting in rare nooks and small quan-

tities; but then I never before was in New Hampshire.

There are three cascades within the circuit of a
mile, all formed by the same winding, rocky-bedded
brook, each one more bewildering than the last, each
one with its ardent, special admirers.

Mrs. Whitney describes the lowest and greatest of
these, in one of the last chapters of "Other Girls,"
better than I could.

Some days we bring our books to some lovely spot
in the woods, and read French and German, while
the thrushes and robins sing overhead. One of the
young men has made us a bower fit for an Oread or
Dryad, in the pine woods below the house, across the
mowing, and past the field of yellow oats. The only
drawback in these haunts is the presence of mosqui-
toes, but we brave them, not seldom, and after our
reading strap up our books with our shawls, take up
our birchen staves, and explore the woody depths,
coming home laden with vines, — gaylium or crow-
foot, — and lately, as the autumn comes on apace,
with gay bunches of purple Michaelmas daisies and
yellow golden-rod.

I must not forget to tell you of our "barn-talks"
before I make an end of this; *symposiums*, I would
call them, if we ever indulged in such long words on

Alstead heights. Mrs. Whitney sometimes takes her writing into one of the barns, and makes a nest for herself in the soft, fragrant hay-heap. She used to keep a dictionary and some books of reference on a little shelf, which one of the boys fixed up for her in the mow, and come out here regularly. We are specially fond of the place on Sunday, when we spend the greater part of the morning here, since there is no church-going until afternoon. We fling the great doors wide, and pile the sweet, fresh hay on the floor, and sit where we can look out upon the picture of waving trees and distant slopes, which the lintels enframe; and where

> "Far off, leaning on each other,
>   Shining hills on hills arise,
> Close as brother leans to brother
>   When they press beneath the eyes
> Of some father praying blessing
>   From the gifts of Paradise."

And we have our best talks here, in the quiet and restfulness which seem peculiarly the atmosphere of this day even in this peaceful land, whither the cares and turmoil of life do not often penetrate as in the busy places of the world. I think the talks are better even than her writings, Edith; I often wish that some of the girls, who have been influenced to higher things by her books, could come to herself with their

questionings and wonderings.   Her faith is so high,
and clear, and sweet.   The blessed words come to
you with a new power in them as she points out their
spiritual meanings. · The girls who love her would be
helped to find out things for themselves, which is the
best kind of helping, after all.

Mrs. Whitney is a beautiful needlewoman, and does
all kinds of work accurately and exquisitely.   To watch
her sew, whether in dress-making or fancy-work, you
would imagine that was the only thing she had ever
tried to do.   You may tell the girls, Edith, that she
never has taught or suggested any occupation, house-
wifely or otherwise, to them, that she is not an adept
in herself.   Her skillful fingers have a wonderful
knack in them, and she isn't apt to undertake anything which she doesn't carry out thoroughly.   This
summer she is crocheting two charming afghans,
taking up now one, then another.   One is all scarlet
and white, the other a "pansy blanket," which is
quite a new idea to me.   The stripes are in the pansy
colors, purple, white, and gold, with a lovely cluster
border in shaded purples.

Now that the evenings are growing longer, and we
cannot play croquet after tea, and it is often too chilly
to sit in the soft, gradual gloaming, so lovely in these
northern latitudes, on the piazza, playing verbal

games, as we used to last month, — proverbs, compara-
tive and superlative, buried cities, and the like, — we
gather round the long table in the dining-room and
its two bright lamps, with our work, some one giving
us scraps of news, and funny bits from the newspapers, freshly arrived by the evening mail. The
advent of the mail at sunset is the great event of the
day. Mrs. —— says we ought to have an artist here
to make a sketch, "Waiting for the Mail." When
nobody happens to drive down to the village, it is
brought up by the postmaster of the Center, who is
likewise the butcher, and rejoices in the inappropriate
name of Shepherd. This double functionary is apt
to linger by the way, Mr. Whitney says, until he has
sold his last shin; so he is often anxiously watched
for ever so long before one or two pairs of sharp and
eager eyes have spied out his slow-paced horse cross-
ing the bridge a mile below us.

We play "crambo" occasionally in the evening,
after the mail excitement is over; and I have a
mind to send you some specimens of our perform-
ance in that line, though I acknowledge that half
the spice is lost, apart from the inspiration and
excitement of the moment which suggests them, and
the fun of the reading aloud to a not over-critical
audience.

Question. — Hadn't the kittens better be drowned?
Word: Gay.

That was what Sarah said in the play
As she came to her master, blithe and gay;
But her master was in a gruesome mood;
Dark, and jealous, and frowning he stood,
And ordered her off.   Poor Pillicoddy!
He was so afraid that his marriage was shoddy!
For his wife's first husband was drowned in the
        sea;
Drowned as dead as a man could be;
But the one dark drop in poor Pilly's cup
Was the fear lest he might some day turn up.
So fancy his feelings when Sarah would say,
With that air so jaunty, and blithe, and gay,
Ever returning upon her round,
— "Hadn't the kittens better be drowned?"
I am something like poor Pillicoddy,
For I'm very sure my verse is shoddy;
And, with Somebody pocketing all the scraps,
I've a haunting fear that some day, perhaps,
Among wise women and wonderful men,
My wretched rhymes may turn up again.
They signify nothing but fury and sound,
And *I* think the kittens had better be drowned!

Question. — Where does the light of a candle go to when it is blown out?

Word : Fly away.

Where does the perfume go when roses fade?
  Where do the songs go when birds fly away?
Where does the day go when earth is in shade?
  Where does the night go when back comes the day?
Where do our thoughts go when we are asleep?
  Where does the sleep go when we are awake?
Where does the ripple go when brooks grow deep?
  Where does the music go when harp-strings break?
I suppose when the birds go, they take their songs too,
  And roses, perhaps, pack up all their perfume.
I can't tell about them ; but I'm certain — ain't you?
  That candle-light goes out in grease-spots and
    gloom.

Last year Mrs. Whitney's birthday was celebrated in grand style here on the fifteenth of September. The night before, all the young people went out into the woods, coming in laden with vines and golden-rod and autumn leaves, glorious branches of them, and turned the house, down stairs, parlor, dining-room, and hall, into a perfect bower, so that when the Lady of the Day stepped from her room in the morning, it seemed like walking in forest glades, she told me, laughing. The day was one long festivity. Every one appeared in the fullest dress they could muster at dinner — ladies in long-trained silks, gentlemen in dress coats, with button-hole bouquets. There was a stunning chicken-pie by way of center-piece, decorated with a gorgeous silken banner, both pie and banner the work of her "own girl's" clever fingers. There were speeches made and healths drunk, and when the elaborate dessert was served, somebody mounted a chair, and read a flaming ode written for the occasion, on what seemed miles of legal cap, tied up with end-less streamers of green and yellow — *why* green and yellow, is not evident. A full-dress croquet party finished up the grand event of the season.

I have a sketch to send you of the dear old house at Milton where Mrs. Whitney lived for many years, and where her children all grew up. It is a sweet, sunny place, midway between the Mill village and the Center; and the pleasant south windows look away to Blue Hills, which bound the horizon. It is a brown, double house, with an L and veranda at the back, a broad piazza in front, with woodbine climbing luxuriantly around its pillars and up the side of the house, — a root of woodbine which her little children brought from Milton woods years ago

MRS. WHITNEY'S HOME, MILTON, MASS.

and planted here. Roses grow about the place in summer, and the turf is very green.

Gnarled old apple trees and dwarf pears abound at the back, and plenty of singing-birds have their habitation among the branches, and in the bird houses, which are perched high up above the tree-tops for their accommodation. Lovely old elms give the place a name — "Elm Corner ;" and I will just whisper a secret to you, Edith : that quaint old house, across the road, is where "Faith Gartney" used to live.

"Faith Gartney" was her first story, you remember, although "Mother Goose for Grown Folks" was the first published book ; and "Elm Corner" is really the home of "We Girls." If you go through the wide hall with its brown furnishings, into the brown and green sitting-room to the right, the ivy and vines in the windows, with their deep cushioned seats, you will surely expect to see "Barbara," and "Rosamond," and "Ruth" come in from the kitchen way, or seated at the round table, or tending their plants. You will look around at the doorway almost sure that "Leslie Goldthwaite" may come in presently for a visit, or that "Stephen Holabird" will be heard halloing, boy-fashion, outside. You see I recall the house as I used to know it. When Mrs. Whitney goes back there to live next winter, it will assume its old familiar aspect again; and we shall all be glad to think of her in the dear old place, where she seems to belong, and where she makes the home brightness.

Doris puts her head in at my door. Her shaker bonnet, trimmed with gray, covers up her golden hair, and makes her look like a bewitching Quakeress. She has a basket on her arm, and a formidable-looking knife in her hand. "Come," she says; "we are all ready to go to the woods and dig ferns. Haven't you finished your letter?" It ought to be finished, by the length of it: so good by, dear Edith. I'll proceed to "back it" now, as the country people up here say. I wonder if you know what that means.

Always affectionately yours, GARRY.

J. T. TROWBRIDGE.

THE home of J. T. Trowbridge, the poet and the story-teller, is a neat brown wooden house, two and a half stories high, situated in a garden of fruit and flowers, on Pleasant Street, in Arlington, Mass.

Close behind it, Arlington Lake, the Spy Pond of historic fame, winds like a broad river for a distance of a mile or more.

A drawing-room, furnished with elegance and taste, occupies the front half of the house, behind which a large dining-room overlooks the pond. From the east window in the upper hall, Bunker Hill monument and the city of Charlestown can be seen, with a glimpse of old Boston itself. From the south-east window of the study, Mount Auburn, the city of the dead, Cambridge observatory, surmounted by the hills of Brighton and Brookline, form an interesting prospect. Arlington Lake, which can be seen from all the windows on the sides and rear of the house, affords a scene of ever-changing variety. A large boat-house belonging to the yacht-club adjoins the grounds of Mr. Trowbridge, who is a prominent member of the association. Many regattas and rowing races start from this house, the upper half of which is fitted with balconies where ladies can sit under shady awnings to encourage the gentlemen contestants with their presence.

In the winter the scene is also busy and animated, for the lake at the time of the ice-harvest is covered with the workmen of Gage & Co., who employ hundreds of men to fill the enormous store-houses on the eastern bank with the ice that supplies distant southern countries as well as the neighboring cities with its cool comfort.

Around this pond, close to the shore, is a narrow path, a favorite walk of Mr. Trowbridge; a shady lane which bounds his garden on the east leads directly to this path. At the highest point of the lane three chesnuts and an oak-tree stand close together, in which pleasant nook he has built a rustic seat where one may sit for meditation, screened from observation by the thick foliage.

His in-door study has many memorials of literary friends, many books presented by the authors with pleasant complimentary sentiments written within.

HOME OF J. T. TROWBRIDGE, ARLINGTON, MASS.

This room is situated on the second floor in the western side of the house, with windows overlooking Pleasant Street and the views already described.

One side of the room is lined with books ; on the opposite is a comfortable sofa.   In the corner stands his desk ; from its top books also occupy the space to the ceiling.

It was in this delightful room that all his well-known series of juvenile books were written, which have become as "familiar as household words" from Maine to California, as well as in England, where they have been widely circulated.   They were begun in *Our Young Folks' Magazine*, and concluded in the *St. Nicholas*, in the following order: " Jack Hazard and his Fortunes," " A Chance for Himself," " Doing his Best," "The Young Surveyor."   " Laurence's Adventures Among the Ice-Cutters, Iron-Workers, Glass-Makers and Ship-Builders," was also written here, together with his irresistible story of " Coupon Bonds," one of the best specimens of Yankee dialect ever written.   The story appeared in the *Atlantic Monthly* for 1865, and has rare dramatic merit, as a version of it, arranged by the writer of this article for the mimic stage, has earned many hundred dollars for charitable purposes, and has been received with shouts of laughter.   The stories which are now collected in a volume with " Coupon Bonds " were also written at this desk.

His " Father Brighthopes " was the earliest of his works, and is still a favorite with young and old. " Neighbor Jackwood " is a novel partly in the Yankee dialect also, and has had a very successful career, being prepared by its author for the stage, where it is still very successful. This novel was written in Paris, where the author experienced the curious sensation of spending his evenings among the fascinations of the gay capital, and his mornings with the New England family of the Jackwoods, which seemed as real as the former to his vivid imagination.

His war-novels were " Cudjo's Cave," "The Three Scouts," and the " Drummer Boy." He also prepared an illustrated work on the South, through which he traveled immediately after the close of the war. He is now preparing a series of illustrated poems for a famous New York publisher. He has already issued two volumes of verse. His poem of " The Vagabonds " has enjoyed great popularity, and is, perhaps, oftener read by elocutionists than any American production ; his " Charcoal Man " and " Darius Green and his Flying Machine " are also favorites These poems, with others, have been read by himself several times in lecture courses.

Our Young Folks Magazine was started in 1865 by Ticknor and Fields, under the editorial charge of Howard M. Ticknor, with Mr. Trowbridge as corresponding editor. In 1870 he became managing editor, and gathered about him a staff of gifted writers which made the magazine popular with young and old, his own serial stories being eagerly read by the parents as well as their children. His sanctum was then in Tremont Street, over Fields & Osgoods' store, a small front room with handsome furniture and carpet, with a bright coal fire in winter, where many a writer of note could be met any fine morning, enjoying the courteous hospitality and wise counsel of the editor.

When engaged upon a prose work, Mr. Trowbridge spends every morning at his desk; but his poems are written whenever the inspiration comes. Many ideas occur to him in the long walks to which he devotes many of his afternoons.

A few winters ago he was passing the head of Mystic Pond, and saw a group of men gathered on the shore, watching a boy whose head was just visible as he struggled in the icy water. He seized a board from the fence, which he broke into two pieces, each about seven feet long. With one foot upon each he pushed out over the cracking ice, against the warnings of the men until he reached the boy, who was just sinking. The ice gave way with the added weight, but he succeeded with great difficulty in pushing the half-frozen boy on one of the boards, and then scrambled out himself, wet and chilled to the bone. For this heroic act he received the medal of the Humane Society for having saved a life. This incident is here cited, against his wish, to show that a poetic talent and taste is not incompatible with energy, courage, and practical use of them.

His son, twelve years old, is taught to row and swim, and seems a model of health and activity; and his daughter, a little, golden-haired fairy about two years old, is a little gleam of sunlight in the home.

In his best stories the author delights in country scenes, and his best interiors are those of rural farmhouses. This taste he seems to have come by naturally, for his father was brought up on a farm in Westmoreland, N. Y., by John Townsend, for whom his son was named. In 1811 the father set out with his household goods in an ox-sled; he crossed the Genessee River, where Rochester now stands, where there was then but one house, and settled at Ogden, eight miles farther west, building a log house, in which the hero of this sketch was born, on the 17th of September, 1827, the youngest but one of a family of nine children.

His father was a fine singer, and a capital story-teller, with a faculty for rhyming his narratives as fast as composed. He died when John was sixteen years old. The son had led the usual life of a farmer's boy, going to school about one half of the year and work-ing hard the rest of the time ; but his heart was not in his work ; his longing for an education was among his earliest recollections, and he used to compose long poems while following the plough, which he would write down by candle-light, in the chimney-corner. At the age of fourteen he studied French and Ger-man from books alone, without the assistance of any one who understood the written language. His favor-ite authors at that time were Byron and Scott.

At the age of eighteen, having had one term in a classical school at Lockport, he went to Illinois, where he read Virgil, and attempted the cultivation of wheat. In this venture he was not successful, partly because he devoted more time to hunting and study than to agriculture. At any rate, he became con-vinced that his genius did not run in that direction, and therefore gave up all idea of becoming a farmer, and determined upon a literary career in spite of all discouragements.

Returning to Lockport he taught school one winter, and perhaps at this place acquired his knowledge of

the workings of the canal-system, which he has since
made such an interesting feature of two of his books.
The next May he set out for New York, alone and
friendless, without a letter of introduction or recom-
mendation of any sort, and with a scanty sum of
money, determined to earn his living by his pen, the
hardest way of earning money in the world, even to
those who have both money and influence.

How his sensitive nature must have been shocked,
and even his brave heart have sunk, before the treatment of many of the self-styled literary men of the
time! While in his country home he had won some
local fame, and his poems and stories had been published in the local papers, but had brought him no
pecuniary reward excepting in one case. He succeeded in winning the prize offered for the best New
Year's Address, by the carriers of the Lockport
paper; but on calling for the promised reward, a book
worth about three dollars, he was told that they could
not afford to give so much, and so they compromised
the matter by paying him $1.50!

After many weary journeys to the upper stories,
where the paper autocrats ruled, he at last found a
friend in Major Noah, of whose kindness and encour-
agement he speaks in the highest terms. He also
discovered the opposite in another well-known editor,

who published a story which the struggling author
ventured to send him. As this article was widely
copied, he modestly asked for his payment, but was
informed that unknown authors were never paid for
their work. This treatment did not discourage him,
although his scanty stock of money was exhausted,
and he was obliged to take refuge in an attic.

At last he found a poor market for his literary
wares in the *Dollar Magazine*, so called from the
price of its subscription, and because it paid its authors at the same rate per page. Even this munificent
payment would not suffice for his maintenance in New
York, and for a short time he laid down the pen to
undertake the engraving of gold pencil-cases at Jersey
City. Not succeeding very well at this business, he
obtained board with a French family, partly for econ-
omy and more for the sake of learning to speak the
language.

About the year 1849 he paid a visit to Boston, where
he decided to remain, as he found the atmosphere
more congenial to his literary taste. Under the *nom
de plume* of "Paul Creyton" he published many articles and one novel. He also was editor in charge of
the *Sentinel*, while its chief was in Washington, in
which he published an article on the Fugitive Slave
Law, which offended many subscribers in the South.
Soon after he published "Father Brighthopes," the

great success of which warranted the publication of
the "Brighthope Series," in four volumes.

In the month of April, 1855, he went to Europe,
where he spent a year, chiefly in England, France and
Italy.   He was one of the original contributors to the
Atlantic Monthly, furnishing for its pages poems, stories, and essays of political and public interest, which
have been very popular, and many of which have
been collected into volumes.

The young people who read this sketch must judge
for themselves from what portion of his varied experience Mr. Trowbridge has gathered the natural incidents which make his stories seem so real.   While
hunting deer in the wilds of Illinois he may have
found a study of "Lord Betterson" in his shingle
palace.   In his hard farm-work he may have met
"Jack Hazard," and "Squire Peternot," and the
inimitable "Ducklow" family.   "George Green-
wood's" struggles in New York, among the editors,
may have recalled the days of his own poverty and of
the time when, penniless and friendless, he never lost
hope, and was too proud to send home for help.

They can learn a lesson of cheerfulness under pri-
vation from his career, and of steady devotion to one
idea which will sooner or later bear the brave worker
to certain success.

One peculiarity of Mr. Trowbridge is his close and

minute observation of even the smallest details of out-
door scenery in his long rambles. Every stone has
for him its sermon, and every brook its open book.
As an elocutionist he avoids the extravagant changes
of tone with which so many readers mar their selec-
tions, and he reads with quiet simplicity of manner
which lends earnestness and force to every expression.
As an editor Mr. Trowbridge was always courteous,
and skillful to detect a pearl even in its rough shell.
His kind advice and assistance have helped many a
bashful genius up the slippery path of fame, and his
genial hospitality and cordial welcome make all
happy who are fortunate enough to visit him in his
home.

MR. J. J. PIATT.
MRS. S. M. B. PIATT.

THE home of these wedded poets is not in the East, where our singers have congregated, but in a romantic and historic section of that region which our parents used to call "out West:" at the present time, to the larger number of Americans, Ohio is in "the East."

North Bend, the town of the poets' residence, is one of the chief historic points in the West. One instantly remembers that it was the home of President Harrison, and that it is his burial-place. His tomb lies only about four hundred yards to the eastward of the Piatt house. To this tomb, a low, whited, brick structure among the cedars, Mrs. Piatt refers in that exquisite child-poem,

HOME OF MR. AND MRS. PIATT, NORTH BEND, OHIO.

A PRESIDENT AT HOME.

I pass'd a President's house to-day —
  "A President, mamma, and what is that?".
Oh, it is a man who has to stay
  Where bowing beggars hold out the hat
For something — a man who has to be
The Captain of every ship that we
Send with our darling flag to the sea —
The Colonel at home who has to command
Each marching regiment in the land.

This President now has a single room,
  That is low, and not much lighted, I fear;
Yet the butterflies play in the sun and gloom
  Of his evergreen avenue, year by year;
And the child-like violets up the hill
Climb, faintly wayward, about him still;
And the bees blow by at the wind's wide will;
And the cruel river, that drowns men so,
Looks pretty enough in the shadows below.

Just one little fellow (named Robin) was there,
  In a red spring vest; and he let me pass
With that charming, careless, high-bred air
  Which comes of serving the great. In the grass
He sat, half-singing, with nothing to do —
No, I did not see the President too :
His door was lock'd (what I say is true).
And he was asleep, and has been, it appears,
Like Rip Van Winkle, asleep for years !

It occupies the top of a lonely ridge which has
been before this, in some dim, pre-historic age, a
place of burial, being what is called an "Indian
mound." Not a few of the neighboring hills are

crowned with these " old pathetic additions." Indeed,
a few miles westward from the Piatt cottage, near the
mouth of the Great Miami, is one of the most extensive works of the mound-builders in the wide West.
They are known as the Fort Hill Embankments.

PRESIDENT HARRISON'S TOMB.

Gen. Harrison believed them to have been used for
military purposes, and he thought that they indicated
superior engineering skill and knowledge. They en-
close eight or ten acres, and are not yet obliterated.
The pioneers of south-eastern Ohio found these embankments overgrown with old forests.

Nearly half a mile farther from the cottage than
the Harrison tomb, and beyond it, stand some old,

romantic ruins of the stone mill which Gen. Harrison built nearly sixty years ago, before he went as Minister to Columbia, South America. It is situated in a deep, lonely hollow among the hills, upon a little stream known as Indian Creek.

A few hundred yards eastward from the tomb, between the hills and the Ohio River, is the site of the North Bend mansion, so famous thirty-five years ago as the "Log Cabin" celebrated in the grand Whig campaign which resulted in the election of Gen. Harrison to the Presidency. The house was, perhaps, partly built of logs ; they were weather-boarded over, however. This historic building was destroyed by fire about twenty years ago. Only a few old orchard trees, including some venerable pear-trees, all of them beautiful in blossom but poor in fruit, together with a small brick office-building, remain to indicate the famous old homestead which, not many years since, was cut up into small lots and sold at public auction.

The Piatt house itself is built at the centre of many beautiful landscapes, the Ohio River being the commanding feature. The cottage stands on the river-line of hills, on the northern (Ohio) side, nearly three hundred feet above the river-level. Every window of the house gives charming river-views — the Ohio southeast and southwest, the Great Miami to the

northward, while from the heights above the house
there is a lovely glimpse of the meeting of the Whitewater with the Miami, reminding one of Tom Moore's
song of "the Vale of Avoca where the bright waters
meet." These gay, sunny waters encircle in their
gleaming arms the most green and fertile of valleys.
In summer the whole country below the dark wooded
heights seems one vast, unbroken, level corn-field.
Across the Ohio to the southward there are also some
delightful Kentucky views — rich and extensive bottom lands, with farm-houses, orchards, pastures, wheat-
fields and corn-fields, bounded by a line of wooded
hills, so that the scene from the upper windows is a
delightful mingling of the idyllic and the romantic.
Evening adds still another fascinating feature to the
landscape. The Ohio & Mississippi R. R. passes
along the foot of the hill in front, while the Indianap-
olis Road winds around the curved river-bank from
above ; and at night the head-lights of the locomo-
tives come flaming toward the house, three or four
miles away, in each direction ; and the whole rocky
hill on which the cottage is built is often jarred with
the long freight-trains.

The Piatt place has been largely left to be the wild
and romantic pleasure-ground which Nature long and
lovingly kept in waiting for the present master and

mistress. The frontage of their little pleasure-ground (two acres in extent) is covered with forest-trees, and slopes down a steep hill to the river. Sitting on the porch you look down through the trees, almost at an angle of forty-five degrees, into the river. Four striking poplar trees, interposing their glimmering, shimmering leaves between one of the windows and a fine water-view, seem to name the place, "The Four Poplars;" but there are those who insist upon calling it "The Thrushes' Nest," which, as Mr. Piatt says, "is very pretty, of course, but hardly modest enough for any of the tenants of the Nest." Since the porch is but twenty feet back from the steep hillside, "Riverbrow" seems the happiest of all the suggested names, though, perhaps, as Mr. Piatt has further remarked, "the designation of a new series of anonymous novels, "No Name," might be a happier one."

The cottage is of wood, a story and a half in height, with French windows in the ends, and in front above. It has a broad porch along the front. The interior is furnished largely, as one would expect, with books. Either on table or shelf, no room misses its share. They take no particular direction; there is poem, novel, essay, history.

Should you chance to stroll into the parlor, you will find a neat and pleasant room, with "Marian's" piano against the wall — "Marian" is the heroine of "The Sad Story of a Little Girl," in WIDE AWAKE, who

> " Beats the piano out of tune,
> And — wants to sleep till noon."

There is, on the wall over the mantel, a portrait in oil of Mrs. Piatt, painted by Theodore Kaufmann, an old German historical painter who lives in Washington. This is fine, as a work of art, but hardly a good or pleasant portrait, being ten years older in looks than its original, and having very little of the tenderness, playfulness and sweetness of her expression, although it has her delicate features, her brow, her dark eyes. A little bust of Longfellow stands on a bracket between the long front windows; and over this hangs an engraving of Ary Schæffer's "Hebe."

Hanging among the engravings and photographs, is a framed autograph letter from Charles Dickens to Mr. Piatt, written a few days before the death of the English novelist; there is, too, a framed portrait-engraving of, and autograph inscription by, Fitz Greene Halleck (the inscription written originally to be placed in a copy of his poems sent to Mrs. Piatt some years before her marriage); and near them is a portrait of Christina Rossetti (whose poems Mr. Piatt admires very much), with an autograph of that remarkable English poetess. Upon the tables are the handsome holiday books of the time ; and doubtless, if you would care to explore one or two scrapbooks, you would find an accumulation of autograph letters from many interesting people, which are, of course, chiefly for private reading.

In the little hall, I may mention, this being Centennial year, that there is a certificate of membership in the " Society of the Cincinnati," signed by George Washington, issued to Mr. Piatt's great-grandfather, who was an original member of that Order, of which Mr. Piatt's father, yet living, is an hereditary member.

What more ? There is a noisy company of little people about the house in all directions — Marian, a tall, dark-eyed little maid of fourteen, is the eldest of the flock. There is Donn, Fred, Guy, and there is the baby, one year old, a bright-faced, bright-haired, blue-eyed, gay, mischievous anonymous, for he has no assured name, although it is presumed to be Louis, with Charles before it.

The mistress of the cottage is a native of Kentucky, born near Lexington. Her maiden name was Sallie M. Bryan (Sarah Morgan Bryan). Her grandfather, Morgan Bryan, was one of several brothers who came into Kentucky with Daniel Boone (Boone's wife was named Rebecca Bryan) from North Carolina.

Mrs. Piatt's early childhood was passed near Versailles, Kentucky, where her mother, a lovely and beautiful woman, died in her own youth, leaving her eldest child, Sarah, only eight years old. The loss of her mother, with various consequent influences, lent to a very delicate and sensitive nature a hue of sadness not easy to outgrow. "The Black Princess," in "A Voyage to the Fortunate Isles," quoted by Mr. Whittier in his "Songs of Three Centuries," was a slave-woman belonging to her grandmother, and was not only her own nurse, but her mother's also, — the feeling in the poem is real and genuine.

Later, she and a younger sister were placed by their father with an aunt, a good and venerable lady still living, Mrs. Boone, a niece by marriage of Daniel Boone, at New Castle, Henry Co., Kentucky. Here she went to school, and was graduated at the Henry Female College, an institution then in charge of a cousin of Charles Sumner. It was here her poetic temperament first manifested itself. She had been always an eager reader, and had especial fondness for Shelley, Coleridge and Byron, though she read Moore and Scott and others of their period.

Some of her early poems were shown by friends to Mr. George D. Prentice, the editor of the *Louisville Journal*, and he praised them, at once recognizing

extraordinary genius. Her early published poems,
appearing in the *Louisville Journal* and *New York
Ledger*, were widely read, widely praised, and were,
perhaps, quite as popular as her later and far superior
work.

It is since her marriage, in June, 1861, that her
more individual characteristics of style have manifested themselves, especially that dramatic element,
so delicate, subtle and strong, which asserts Mrs.
Piatt's intellectual kinship with Mrs. Elizabeth Barrett
Browning, and with her only — they stand together
in a splendid solitude, the royal sisters.

Mrs. Piatt is slightly above the medium height for
a woman, with a delicate and rather fragile appearance, very graceful in carriage and figure. Her head
is singularly fine in shape and outline. She has
dark, tender, hazel eyes, under finely-arched brows,
a small, sensitive and proud mouth, a straight, well-
shaped nose. Her hair, silk-like in fineness, is of the
real auburn hue, brown in the shadow, golden in the
sunlight.

Although many things have touched her life with
sadness, and she is too often melancholy, she is, after
all, in her own house, full of girlish lightness and
playfulness. Not disliking, but enjoying, society, she
can live without it with perfect cheerfulness. For

weeks at a time, in bad weather, "Riverbrow" is almost inaccessible; but Mrs. Piatt finds ample entertainment in her household, her household duties, and herself.

Mrs. S. M. B. Piatt.

At home she is apparently as little of the literary woman as it is possible to be, and one might dine at the cottage from one New Year until the next without suspecting his hostess of active authorship. She has no regular hours for writing, and cannot be persuaded to make it the aim and business of her life. Her poems are written out-of-doors if possible. Her composition is rapid, — some of her most finished poems have been written at one sitting.

It is striking evidence of her lack of personal literary ambition, that every poem of hers that has been published since her marriage has been copied and given to the public by the hands of her husband, who, most happily for us, has had a good deal of ambition for her. To Mr. Piatt we owe the pleasure of her books. Her own hand would never have collected her poems. Her first book was " The Nests at Washington," published in New York, in 1864, the larger part being Mr. Piatt's poems. Her next volume was " A Woman's Poems " (Boston, 1871). Her last book was " A Voyage to the Fortunate Isles " (Boston, 1874). A new volume is in preparation.

Her daily life is devoted, patiently and happily, to her household cares, and to her children. As a Southerner, before her marriage, her people having been slave-holders, she had slight experience in domestic matters, and none of the training which falls to the lot of Northern women. But with all her cares she has taught her children to read and write, and has instructed them largely in all their early lessons. Her many poems referring to children have been

nearly always suggested by real children, — their
genuine questions and remarks are often given nearly
word for word.

Happy with her "foolish yellow-heads " — the five,
Marian, Donn, Fred, Guy and baby — there is still a
sob, suddenly, in nearly all the poems. I think the
Rachel-sorrow never found such powerful expression
elsewhere. There are graves of her own on "the
beautiful burial hill," — two. Here the mother count:

"How many graves are in this world?"   "Oh, child,"
    His mother answered, "surely there are two."
Archly he shook his pretty head and smiled :
    "I mean in this whole world, you know I do."

"Well, then, in this whole world : in east and west,
    In north and south, in dew and sand and snow,
In all sad places where the dead may rest :
    There are two graves — yes, there are two, I know."

"But graves have been here for a thousand years, —
    Or, for ten thousand?   Soldiers die, and kings ;
And Christians die — sometimes."   "My own poor tears
    Have never yet been troubled by these things.

.   .   .   "More graves within the hollow ground, in sooth,
    Than there are stars in all the pleasant sky? —
Where did you ever learn such dreary truth,
    Oh, wiser and less selfish far than I?

"I did not know, — I who had light and breath :
    Something to touch, to look at, if no more.
Fair earth to live in, who believe in death,
    Till, dumb and blind, he lies at their own door?

. . . "I did not know — I may have heard or read —
Of more ; but should I search the wide grass through,
Lift every flower and every thorn," she said,
"From every grave — oh, I should see but two ! "

Two years ago the family came home from a long
stay in Washington, one evening in summer, July 3d,
glad, father and mother and children, to reach the
fresh, green, fragrant spot, after a tedious and dusty
journey. Gayest of all was the little eldest son, Victor,
a gentle, lovely boy, especially attached to his mother.
He had a merry day on the morrow, "the Fourth."
Just at dusk, as his father came home from the city,
he was playing with some powder which he had stored
in a bottle, when it exploded — and the same in-
stant the little fellow ran toward them crying assur-
ingly, "Mamma, I am not hurt much ! I am not hurt,
mamma ! " But the next moment he was no longer
with them.

The master of the cottage was born in Dearborn
County, Indiana, hardly thirty-five miles away from
his present home. At fourteen years of age he was
placed by his father in charge of an uncle, who was
then publisher of the *Ohio State Journal*, at Columbus,
to learn the printer's trade. At this time another and
smaller boy was there exercising himself in the art
and mystery of types ; this smaller lad was William
D. Howells. Some years later they fell together

again.   One evening Mr. Piatt, who had in the interim been in Louisville, Kentucky, some months, and had tried his wings in various flights of verse through the *Louisville Journal*, came into the editorial rooms of the *Ohio State Journal*, which had by this time passed into the hands of new publishers, for the purpose of looking for a copy of Mr. Prentice's paper.

The " smaller boy " of yore was there, now one of the editors.   He at once recognized his boyish friend, and renewed the acquaintance.   Mr. Howells, too, published verses, in the *National Era*, and elsewhere.   The mutual tastes and aspirations drew them together ; and, as a consequence, at Christmas, 1859, there appeared a modest little volume, " Poems of Two Friends."

Mr. Piatt has spent a goodly share of his time in Washington, having been appointed to a place in the Treasury Department by Mr. Salmon P. Chase, the late Chief Justice, a few days after the latter became Secretary of the Treasury.   While in Louisville, he had met the young Kentucky poetess, and now they were married, during Mr. Piatt's first year in Washington.   In that city, and in Georgetown, they lived for some years during the war.

In 1868 these mated singing-birds fixed their nest in the rocky eyrie at North Bend, Mr. Piatt having become an editor of one of the Cincinnati papers. In 1870, however, he was recalled to Washington, where, as Librarian of the House of Representatives,

MR. JOHN J. PIATT.

he has remained during sessions of Congress, his family being with him several winters. Recently, owing to the political change in the *personale* of the House, a new Librarian being appointed, Mr. Piatt is again at North Bend, and has resumed journalistic labor.

Personally, Mr. Piatt is one of the young modern men, keen and clear-cut, both in appearance and action.

His poems have appeared in three volumes, besides "Poems of Two Friends." "Nests at Washington" (New York, 1864) was named from some great bomb-shells before the White House, into whose

> . . . "hollow horror
> Flew tenderest summer wings!
>
> "Deep in the awful chambers
> Of the gigantic Death,
> The wrens their nests had builded,
> And dwelt with loving breath."

"Western Windows" was published in New York in 1869, and "Landmarks" in 1872.

The life of the early West, of the pioneers, and the experiences of the rude farmer, have taken a strong hold on the sympathies and the imagination of Mr. Piatt; his poems are set, as with pictures, with Ohio valley landscapes; and

> . . . "through the dust of long ago,
> Creep the Pennsylvania wagons up the twilight — white and
> slow."

Many of them are finished idyls, and far more distinctively American than the "dialect-poems" of Hay and Bret Harte. For instance, there is the poem, "Riding to Vote." Translated into any language, its American flavor would still be pungent and unmistakable:

"In Jackson's days a gay young man, with spirit hale and blithe
And form like the young hickory, so tough and tall and lithe,
I first remember coming up — we came a wagon-load,
A dozen for Old Hickory — this rough November road."

A man's thought, expressed with a woman's grace and sweetness, is embodied in

ROSE AND ROOT.

A FABLE OF TWO LIVES.

The Rose aloft in sunny air,
　Beloved alike by bird and bee
Takes for the dark Root little care
　That toils below it ceaselessly.

I put my question to the flower:
　Pride of the summer, garden queen,
Why livest thou thy little hour?
　And the Rose answered, "I am seen."

I put my question to the Root —
　"I mine the earth content," it said,
"A hidden miner underfoot;
　I know a Rose is overhead."

Life passes very pleasantly at "Riverbrow," as in Arcadia, when the family are all at home; there are excursions on the wooded hill-slopes, readings and picnicings in the green shade ; there are strolls by the river, drives through the valleys of the Miami and Whitewater ; in good weather refined and genial society is within reach — in short, quite their share of earthly happiness has been vouchsafed to the inmates of "Riverbrow."

EDGAR FAWCETT.

THOSE who know Edgar Fawcett as a writer for children are few compared with the larger audience that he addresses through his novels, tales and poems. His first book, however, published in 1871, under the title of "Short Poems for Short People," was essentially a work of juvenile character. Its fate was like that of most "first books," and the obscurity of the publishers who brought it out possibly contributed towards its non-success. But since then Mr. Fawcett has written many delightful poems for young people, and these he purposes adding, at some future time, to the "Short Poems" already mentioned. There is little doubt that this second and greatly revised edition will some day be very popular; for, during the past three years or so, Mr. Fawcett's graceful naturalness, and fragrant

humor, have won him scores of little friends through
out the country.

Edgar Fawcett was born in New York city, and is
now in his thirtieth year.   In 1867 he graduated from

EDGAR FAWCETT.

Columbia College, and has since then not only made
literature his profession, but has shown himself one
of the most industrious magazine-writers of the day.
Tales and poems have flowed from his pen with great
rapidity.   It may almost be said that scarcely a week
passes without his name appearing in some periodical

before the public. He is also the author of two novels, "Purple and Fine Linen," published by Carleton & Co. in 1873, and "Ellen Story," published last year by E. J. Hale & Son, of New York. The last book has won for him high praise, as a work of rare charm and undoubted power.

But industry and versatility, only too often, as we know, accompany feebleness, or at least carelessness of composition. It is but justice to Mr. Fawcett to say that everything which he writes bears in a most striking degree the marks of thorough artistic care. A slip-shod rhyme, or an ill-constructed sentence, are unknown amid his work. Not long ago he showed the writer a letter addressed to him by an eminent American poet, in which the following words occurred : "Whence come such intellectual power and constancy to your work, that you are enabled to compose novels, prose sketches, long poems and short, in so limited a period of time ? And then the art of these pieces is always so admirable !"

Surely this is rare praise ; but those most familiar with Mr. Fawcett's writings must admit it to be well-deserved.

In stature Mr. Fawcett is of medium height, and his figure inclines a trifle toward stoutness. His face is mobile, and of an ever-varying expressive power.

In conversation he is remarkable for a polished ease, a readiness of phrase, and the occasional play of a delicate, fanciful humor. All acknowledge his great attractiveness of manner, and to spend an hour in his society is to deal afterward in some very pleasant intellectual memories.

Mr. Fawcett has lived the life of cities. He is a man of the world, in the fullest, broadest sense. Unlike most poets, he is full of self-possession, and trained to the utmost in all social niceties. The close observation of nature constantly shown in his poems would suggest one who has lived a rural life ; but with the exception of passing his summers at a country-place, Mr. Fawcett is as entirely metropolitan in his general mode of living as anyone to be found in the great, populous city where he resides.

He is still unmarried. His love for children is sincere and profound, and he possesses a power of amusing them that his many young admirers will readily understand. Especially does he excel in the weaving of those long, delightful fairy "rigmaroles" in which, as the children would say, "he makes it up as he goes along." Many of his best juvenile poems have been published anonymously. We are tempted to quote the following, because it shows the author's exquisite power of pleasing his little readers by the

most simple, natural, and truthful means. A little
girl, we should imagine, is supposed to be addressing
some farm-servant :

THE MURDERED KITTENS.

I won't believe it of you, John ;
   You never, never could be
Such an awfully heartless kind of wretch
   It is very clear to me !

I saw you ugly to Bruno once,
   And whip old lame Bobbin, too ;
But drown four poor little kittens ? No,
   I will *not* believe it of you !

Why, John, could you go and stand there now,
   And hear the old cat's wild cries,
And let her rub herself on your leg,
   And lift up her great, sad eyes ?

Could you do all this, I ask of you, John
   (And I ask without one bit of mirth),
If you'd just been sweeping her family
   From off the face of the earth ?

And haven't you too much sense to believe
   (Why, the mere thought makes me frown !)
That kittens were ever created, John,
   Just for cruel people to drown ?

You and I were born that we might grow up
   Live our lives and be this or that ;
And in the same way is each kitten meant
   To become a developed cat !

And to kill one is simply a horrid sin!
  A deed most awful to do!
So, if anyone has drowned the kittens, John,
  I cannot believe 'twas you!

Different in its way, yet possessing much of the
author's peculiarly quaint charm, is the following :

GETTING PHOTOGRAPHED.

And so I must sit in this chair and keep still?
  I'll try, though I'm only real still when asleep.
(What's mamma gone away for?   I've got quite a chill ;
  Yes, truly; my flesh is beginning to creep!

O gracious! he's hiding behind that queer thing!
  I don't know what name it has, though mamma said
Suppose it should all of a sudden go *ping!*
  And leave me to sit here without any head!

Dear me, here he comes again!)   Place my arm so?
  Stop creasing my forehead? and fix my eyes there?
(He treats me as if I were made out of dough!
  And—what *is* he putting against my back hair?

Now he's hiding behind that queer thing once again.)
  Your behavior is certainly puzzling, dear sir.
I declare, I consider it positive pain
  Sitting here like a poker, forbidden to stir.

It will not be long, did you say?   Can I wink?
  Very well; I'm quite ready, and won't move at all.
(This man has the crossest expression, I think,
  And then,—am I sure that mamma's within call?)

O my! Has he done? Is it time now to go?
　Getting photographed doesn't take long, I admit.
Mamma, please don't call me the worst goose you know,
　But — I thought it would *hurt*, just a wee little bit!

Irresistibly funny, too, are these lines. How many
a child can recall just such an experience :

LEARNING TO MILK.

Timothy, let me milk the cow.
　Now, Timothy, please do!
Of course you're in a hurry, sir,
　Because I'm asking you.

I haven't tried in such an age
　To milk her — that you know!
Ah, nice old Tim! I thought you would!
　How do you do it? So?

It really is the queerest thing!
　My hands feel firm and strong,
But though I pull the same as you,
　I always do it wrong.

I might explain it, Tim, you know,
　Were all my fingers thumbs.
How is it that I strain and strain,
　And no milk ever comes?

Ah! here's a drop! Hurrah! hurrah!
　I'm milking! Don't you see?
But then, why *does* she gush for you,
　And trickle, Tim, for me?

Just watch this little dribbling stream,
  So miserably thin !
I wonder if she's obstinate,
  And likes to hold it in ?

Perhaps she won't be milked by me,
  A mere child, not thirteen.
And yet I somehow *can't* believe
  A cow *could* act so mean !

In marked contrast to the preceding verses, are
these deliciously tender ones :

TWO KINDS OF LOVE.

Yes, mamma loves me with all her heart,
  And the same way I love mamma.
But gracious ! how very different,
  Each from each, those two loves are !

Shall I tell you what her love is like ?
  I think it's as if God chose
To have made her a rose-bush, large and green,
  With only me for a rose.

Or as if she'd been a robin, with just
  One birdling to keep from cold ;
Or a space of sweet, fresh grass, with one
  Little dandelion of gold.

Or as if she'd been a dull, wild land,
  With a single frail young tree ;
Or a sky with a single star to hold,—
  That's about how mamma loves me.

Fancy now, that I were the rose, you know,
  The dandelion, the star,
Or the nestling bird that I told you of,—
  And that's how I love mamma.

The above poems are only taken at random from over a hundred such that Mr. Fawcett has written during the past few years. There can be no doubt of their merit. Mr. Fawcett has encountered, among critical friends, not a little opposition to the idea of his writing these dainty juvenile scraps. "They will spoil your reputation as a poet and novelist," has been more than once said to him. "I hope not," he once smilingly answered; "but even if such awful consequences follow I shall continue my bad habit."

We hope that all the young Wide Awakes agree with us in hoping sincerely that Mr. Fawcett will abide by his excellent resolution.

JAMES RUSSELL LOWELL.

ABOUT half a mile west from Harvard Square in Cambridge, and adjoining on one side the beautiful cemetery of Mount Auburn, is Elmwood, the home of one of the best-known of American poets.

The approach to the grounds is through a narrow lane which branches off on the left from the main street, — Brattle Street, as it is called, on which, as you may chance to remember, the poet Longfellow resides. The stately mansion stands on high ground, and on every side it is hemmed in by tall elms, so that, in the summer-time especially, it is almost impossible for one to catch a full glimpse of it until he has arrived very near.

The house, though a century old, shows no signs of decay. It was built by master-builders, and by a

ELMWOOD. — THE HOME OF MR. LOWELL.

famous generation whose good nature still lingers in the fine large rooms, and the capacious chimneys.

If you should seek to know something of its history you would be told that the mansion was first occupied by Thomas Oliver — by whom also it was erected — the last royal lieutenant-governor of the Province of Massachusetts. At the outbreak of the revolutionary war the owner returned to England, and the house then became the property of Elbridge Gerry, one of the signers of the Declaration of Independence, governor of Massachusetts, and Vice-President of the United States.

After the death of Mr. Gerry the estate was purchased by the Rev. Charles Lowell, father of the poet, by whom it was greatly improved, and most of the trees now towering around it were planted by him, also the name of "Elmwood" was bestowed on the estate.

In this house, on the 22d of February, 1819, James Russell Lowell was born. In 1838 he was graduated at Harvard College where his father and grandfather had graduated before him. In his "Indian Summer Reverie" he thus pleasantly alludes to his academic career :

" Though lightly prized the ribboned parchments there,
Yet, *collegisse juvat*, I am glad

That here what colleging was mine I had, —
It linked another tie, dear native town, with thee."

At the time of his graduation Mr. Lowell was a young man of nineteen years, full of life and promise, and as yet undecided as to his future course. It was supposed by some of his friends that he might follow the example of his father and become a minister. On the contrary he chose law, was in due time admitted to the bar, and, finally, opened an office in Boston.

A great lawyer has recently remarked that whoever seeks to render himself famous in the profession of the bench and bar, must first learn to "eat sawdust without butter." This is a somewhat inelegant but forcible way of expressing the fact that a young lawyer has a hard road to travel, and that, at first, he must neither expect much patronage nor grumble because his outgoes exceed his income.

Mr. Lowell had the advantage of very many other men of his age, in that his pecuniary circumstances were sufficiently easy to enable him to live without much worry or fret. Nevertheless, he ere long arrived at the conviction that he and the law had but little in common, and that the sooner he abandoned it the better off he would be in the end.

On a lucky day, therefore, he forsook his sheepskin

volumes, and the few clients he had managed to attract, and went back to his other books, and the green trees of Elmwood, with the new resolve of leading henceforth a purely literary life.

He had already tried his skill in the art of versification, and had written several poems of more than common interest. In 1841, as a first venture, he published a small volume of poems, entitled "A Years' Life," which, three years later, was followed by another volume, with the title of "The Legend of Brittany, Miscellaneous Poems and Sonnets."

Meanwhile he had fallen in love, and in 1844 was married to Miss Maria White, of Watertown, a most excellent and highly esteemed lady, and a poetess also, whose early death, in 1853, was the occasion of that beautiful and familiar poem of Mr. Longfellow's, beginning :

> "Two angels, one of Life and one of Death,
>   Passed o'er the village as the morning broke;
> The dawn was on their faces, and beneath
>   The sombre houses hearsed with plumes of smoke,"

and thus continues :

> "'Twas at thy door, O friend, and not at mine,
>   The angel with the amaranthine wreath,
> Pausing, descended, and with voice divine,
>   Whispered a word that had a sound like Death."

This poem of the "Two Angels" has long been a favorite, though by many misinterpreted. In order to correct an error it may be said here that the coming of the Angel of Life is an allusion to the birth of one of Mr. Longfellow's children, which was coincident with the death of his friend's genial wife.

In 1845 Mr. Lowell published a volume of prose essays entitled "Conversations on some of the Old Poets," which have always been regarded as among the very best of his writings, and as one of the best of helps to the student of English poetry. Three years later came another volume of poems, then another, and finally, in 1848, the pleasant and sparkling poem called "A Fable for Critics."

This "Fable," I fancy you already know, is a sort of review in verse of American poets. Very many of the writers of his day are summoned before him to have their portraits taken, and then dismissed, usually with a sharp rap or two on the knuckles. The production is very witty and humorous, and for the most part is written in a spirit of genial appreciation.

In the same appeared also "The Biglow Papers," a poetical satire upon the invasion of Mexico by the United States, the state of the slavery question, etc. These verses first appeared in the newspapers, and it is safe to say that no productions of a similar char-

acter in this country were ever half so popular.
Everybody read them, and laughed over their Yankee
wit and humor. One of the learned critics of the day
was so attracted by them that he advised their author
to renounce imaginative poety and henceforth confine
himself to making fun of the follies and foibles of his
fellow men.

In 1851–2 the poet made a first visit to Europe ;
and, on returning home delivered a course of lectures
on English poetry before the Lowell Institute, in
Boston.

In the spring of 1855 Mr. Longfellow resigned his
professorship of *Belles Lettres* in Harvard College,
and Mr. Lowell was appointed as his successor.
From this time onward he has held this position, has
written new books of prose and poetry, and been
editor of the *Atlantic Monthly* and the *North American Review.*

Whoever wishes to become somewhat familiar with
the poet's home must first look through the collected
edition of his poetry, for it is a memorable fact that
very many of his best pieces have been suggested by
the scenery surrounding his abode, and particularly
the leafy patriarchs which swing and cast shadows
before his study windows.

As you near the house there is one tree which

always arrests the attention of a stranger. A very
tall elm it is, though in recent years its towering
height has been noticeably diminished by the worms,
which have little sympathy with things beautiful. It
is of this giant object that the poet writes in " A Day
in June : "

> "And one tall elm, this hundreth year
> Doge of our leafy Venice here,
> Who, with an annual ring doth wed
> The blue Adriatic overhead,
> Shadows with his palatial mass
> The deep canals of flowing grass,
> Where glow the dandelions sparse,
> For shadows of Italian stars."

Other poems there are which assist the reader in
forming a clear idea of Elmwood and its surroundings. Looking out through his study windows the
poet may discern the "silver Charles " winding slug-
gishly through slopes and meadows, distant farms, the
blue hills of Milton, and what he himself calls the
" Coptic Tombs : "

> "Below, the Charles, — a stripe of nether sky,
>   Now hid by rounded apple-trees between,
> Whose gaps the missplaced sail sweeps bellying by,
>   Now flickering golden through a woodland screen,
> Then spreading out, at his next turn beyond,
>   A silver circle, — like an inland pond —
> Steps seaward silently through marshes purple and green.

"Dear marshes! vain to him the gift of sight
   Who cannot in their various incomes share,
From every season drawn, of shade and light,
   Who sees in them but levels brown and bare;
Each change of storm or sunshine scatters free
   On them its largess of variety,
For Nature, with cheap means, still works her wonders rare.

"In spring they lie one broad expanse of green,
   O'er which the light winds run with glimmering feet;
Here, yellower stripes track out the creek unseen,
   There, darker growths o'er hidden ditches meet,
And purpler stains show where the blossoms crowd,
   As if the silent shadows of a cloud
Hung there becalmed, with the next breath to fleet."

Adjoining the grounds of Elmwood, as I have said, is the beautiful city of the dead, Mount Auburn. Screened by its loveliness and its silent watch are two of the poet's children and his first wife. On the grave of his first-born he wrote that sweet, tender poem called "The First Snow," of which a few stanzas must be given here:

"The snow had begun in the gloaming,
   And busily, all the night
Had been heaping field and highway
   With a silence deep and white.

*   *   *   *   *   *   *   *

"I stood and watched by the window
   The noiseless work of the sky,
And the sudden flurries of snow-birds,
   Like brown leaves whirling by.

" I thought of a mound in sweet Auburn
   Where a little headstone stood,
How the flakes were folding it gently,
   As did robins the babes in the wood.

" Up spoke our own little Mabel,
   Saying, 'Father, who makes it snow?'
And I told of the good All-Father,
   Who cares for us all below.

" Again I looked at the snow-fall,
   And thought of the leaden sky
That arched o'er our first great sorrow,
   When that mound was heaped so high.

" I remember the gradual patience
   That fell from the cloud like snow,
Flake by flake, healing and hiding
   The scar of that deep-stabbed woe.

" And again to the child I whispered,
   ' The snow that husheth all,
Darling, the merciful Father
   Alone can make it fall!'"

" Then with eyes that saw not I kissed her,
   And she, kissing back, could not know
That my kiss was given to her sister,
   Folded close under deepening snow."

One of the most popular of Mr. Lowell's poetic
productions is, perhaps, the brightest thing in the
" Biglow Papers," — a poem which, if you remember,
Parson Wilbur calls a " pastoral," but which the
poet himself calls " The Courtin'."

Just after the election of General Taylor to the

presidency of the United States, a certain room in one of the hotels at Washington was crowded with rude men who had assembled there to discuss politics in general and the prospects of sundry office-seekers in particular. While the jargon was at its height a roughly-clad son of New England came into the room, and, addressing the company, exclaimed:

"Who says there are no American poets?"

It was a strange question, strangely put before such a gathering. The rude men pondered, but nobody ventured either to dispute or to assent to the interrogation.

The New Englander went on to say:

"Well, if anybody says there ain't I'm prepared to dispute him. *I* have found an American poet. I don't know who he is, nor where he lives; but he is the author of these lines, and he is a poet."

He then took a newspaper from his coat-pocket, and, with proper emphasis and gesture, proceeded to read:

> 'Zekle crep' up, quite unbeknown,
>   An' peeked in thru the winder;
> An' there set Huldy all alone,
>   'Ith no one nigh to hinder.
>
> "Agin' the chimbly crooknecks hung,
>   An' in amongst 'em rusted

The queen's arm that gran'ther Young
    Fetched back from Concord busted.

"The wannut logs shot sparkles out
    Towards the pootiest, bless her!
An' leetle fires danced all about
    The chiny on the dresser.

"The very room, coz she was in,
    Looked warm frum floor to ceilin',
And she looked full as rosy agin
    Ez the apples she was peelin'.

"She heerd a foot an' knowed it, tu,
    A-raspin' on the scraper, —
All ways to once her feelins' flew
    Like sparks in burnt up paper.

"He kin' o' litered on the mat,
    Some doubtfle of the seekle;
His heart kep goin' pity pat,
    But hern went pity Zekle."

Doubtless, many another anecdote of a similar sort
might be related, as showing how speedily Mr.
Lowell's verse, especially when it is brimming over
with cheerful humor, finds its way into a crowd and
takes full possession of the popular heart. Safely,
indeed, may he be called a "poet of the people,"
since few other American writers have had the fortune
to see so many of their productions leading a sort of
Bohemian life in the newspapers, devoid of the trace
of their authorship!

Of late years the poet has been something of a politician, not unmindful, perhaps, that one of the greatest of English bards, the renowned author of " Paradise Lost," did not think himself justified in keeping aloof from the political circles of his day.

Before the beginning of the civil war he was thoroughly an abolitionist, and labored with other of his friends to bring about the emancipation of the slave. This fact did not, as many might have fancied, make him any enemies in the South. Hence one would say that he is "just such a politician as Milton was, and will never narrow himself down to any other party than one which includes all mankind within its lines."

We will now, if you please, go into the native home of the poet. Until within a few years his study was on the third floor, in that corner of the mansion on which, in the engraving, the light falls so pleasantly.

Leaving the gateway behind we first ascend the walk, which, at a distance of about one hundred yards, leads up to the broad stone steps before the entrance. You perceive at once that the poet is a "lover of the light," for ·the first object that you encounter on your visit is a huge glass door — or rather a huge glass window which serves as a door, — through which you may gaze into the hall, through and out again by another glass door into the leafy perspective beyond.

On the right of the hall, as you have entered, is a drawing-room furnished in the rich and solid old-fashioned style. We will not linger here, but at once pay our respects to the poet in the room on the left of the hall.

This is the "study," a grand room in every respect, and as cozy and comfort-giving as it is grand. It is not just like going into an ancient interior, to be sure; but you feel, as soon as the door rolls back upon its hinges, that you are treading a floor into which nothing of the new style can ever find entrance.

A bright fire is burning on the hearth — and such a hearth! A great square hole in the chimney, polished dog-irons, on which are piled the crackling logs, bright beneath and black overhead, — just such a place as the Christmas saint would wish to lurk in if benumbed on a frosty morning. Well, I dare say you may have seen such a hearth, away back in the country, but rarely in the crowded houses of our cities.

On the mantel-shelf is a bronze clock, which would fain conceal its richness under a crystal globe. On either side are vases, Gettysburg relics, and other curiosities. On the right of the shelf, and where the

room projects back, forming a sort of alcove, stands a card-table of solid mahogany and old-fashioned origin, about which, it is averred, some of the renowned Cambridge worthies, of several generations gone by, used to smile and gossip over a game of whist. It came into the poet's possession by a mere accident ; and where you see it now you will probably see it a good many years hence, for it is rarely used now-a-days.

Near the table, and on the north side of the room are book-shelves, laden with treasures which years have brought together. On the south side are other shelves, in like manner, displaying a wealth of fine bindings, mostly of foreign workmanship. In the south-east corner of the room is an old-fashioned secretary-desk, which the poet resorts to only on rare occasions.

In the centre of the room is the study-table, strewn with books, manuscripts, letters, and almost everything else that falls within a poet's fancy, Near the inkstand, and with its mouth-piece well nigh concealed beneath a cluster of quills, is a huge meerschaum pipe, whose sombre hue bespeaks many a " well spent hour among the clouds."

Whether at work or at leisure, Mr. Lowell occupies the broad easy-chair which, as you perceive, stands midway between the table and the fire-place. In this chair he has done most of his writing, his only desk being a stiff piece of paste-board, conveniently resting on his knee.

One would fancy that he must oftentimes suffer from an aching back, or feel at times as if his neck were going to break asunder. He is never troubled either way ; and if you were to ask him how he came to invent so singular a substitute for a desk he would answer that he has always made use of such a contrivance, and cannot accustom himself to any other.

So there he sits and dreams, and when the Muse inspires him plans and writes out good thoughts for his fellow men, glancing up across at the few pictures which hang upon the walls, or perhaps turning half around, to scan the silver Charles as on he winds by marsh and meadow.

Such is the poet's "study" as it is to-day. Through the door which opens on the left of the fire-place you may enter another study which, in other years, was occupied by the poet. Books crowd the walls on all sides, a few portraits hang here and there, and in the centre of the room is a square desk, which, like the more old-fashioned desk in the adjoining room, is rarely used. The only "curiosity" in the room which rivets your attention is a pair of silver sleeve-buttons, now tarnished almost into blackness, which were once worn by Robert Burns

J. R. Lowell

Mr. Lowell is thoroughly a lover of his home. Here he was born, and here he will remain, probably, until the end of life. On a spring or summer day you may often see him out in his garden as a *practical* lover of nature, and proving to all his neighbors that a poet may also be something of a horticulturist.

He is fond of trees and flowers, and spends much of his time associated with them. He is fond, also, of the rifle and rod, and not unfrequently has he been discovered lurking in wilder regions than his own peaceful Elmwood, equipped with the sportman's ardor and arms. As a pedestrian, too, he is not less noted among those who have an opportunity of seeing him in his daily life.

He never rides when he can walk, and he always walks be the weather what it may, when time and circumstances permit. Few men of his age enjoy better health, are more erect in their bearing, or more robust and manly in their appearance than Mr. Lowell. I have often seen him in the bleakest of wintry weather walking leisurely through Cambridge thoroughfares with not even the ghost of an overcoat upon his back, and as often have I said to myself, "Surely, you will be a sufferer from this." But no, in winter or summer, spring or autumn, he is always the same, and goes back and forth as if wearing the armor of Achilles.

Socially, the poet is one of the most affable and genial men that have ever lived. Always agreeable and pleasant as a conversationalist; always polite; always honest and honorable in his intercourse with his fellow-men, he charms most those who know him best, while those who know him least never deny him that respect which is born of true friendship.

One always leaves Elmwood with a feeling of regret; for to pass from its cozy and quiet interior, its green trees, its flowers and song of birds, out into the broad highway, noisy with the tread of many feet, and the tinkling of horse-car bells, is just like going from a realm of imagination into a world of reality. A hundred rods leads you from the country, as it were, into the city. Your poet's dream vanishes. You almost forget where you have been in the last hour; and thus you slip back into your old ways, and the duties of life again crowd upon you.

BAYARD TAYLOR.

PENNSYLVANIA is far more famous for coal
and iron than for poetry, for out of the hundred and sixty or seventy poets who figure in the last
edition of Dr. Griswold's "Poets and Poetry of America" only twelve were born in that State. But among
these was Joseph Hopkinson, who wrote our national
anthem, "Hail Columbia." Then came George P.
Morris, who wrote "Woodman, spare that tree,"
and other songs which Dr. Griswold thought nearly
faultless. Then came Robert T. Conrad, commonly
called Judge Conrad, who wrote a play about Jack
Cade, for Edwin Forrest. Then Henry B. Hirst,
who wrote a poem about Endymion, and Mr. Thomas
Dunn English, who wrote the pretty song of "Ben
Bolt." These, and three lesser writers whom I need
not name, bring us down to about fifty-five years ago,
when real poets began to appear in Pennsylvania, —

for Hopkinson and Morris and Conrad were not
poets, but clever writers of verse. Four came within
four years, one in each succeeding year, — Thomas
Buchanan Read in 1822, George H. Boker in 1823,
Charles G. Leland in 1824, and Bayard Taylor in
1825. Two were born in Philadelphia, and two in
Chester county. The last two were Buchanan Read
and Bayard Taylor.

Bayard Taylor was born at Kennett Square, Chester County, on January 11, 1825. I know the old
house in which he and his brothers and sisters were
born : two girls, who are now mothers, with boys and
girls of their own, and four sons, one of whom was
slain at Gettysburg as he was leading his men to
battle. A brave soldier and a good man was Colonel
Frederick Taylor. But I must not tell the story of
his life, or the story of the lives of the other Taylor children. My business is to tell the readers
of WIDE AWAKE, about Bayard Taylor. He is
descended from one Robert Taylor, a primitive
Quaker and a companion of William Penn, who settled
at Kennett Square a hundred and ninety-six years ago,
and from a Lutheran clergyman who emigrated from
Southern Germany about fifty years later. Bayard Taylor was the fourth child, three having died before his
birth, and it was doubtful for a time whether he was
destined to live, he was so weak and frail.

He was sensitive as most delicate children are ; he disliked rough sports, and was a mystery to other children, who did not understand his tastes, and could not sympathize with his little ambitions. He began to read poetry as soon as he could read at all, say when he was five or six years old, and was deeply impressed by the death of two great poets who died in his seventh year, and by their biographies in the newspapers. One was Sir Walter Scott, the other was the German poet Goethe, whose "Faust" he was one day to render into English verse. He struggled into rhymed couplets at this early age, and two or three years later succeeded in writing whole stanzas. Many other children have done the same and yet have grown up as prosaic as the most practical of parents could wish; but when a child who writes verse is what the others are not—a born poet, he goes on writing verse to the end of his days. A poet sings as naturally as a bird, but, unlike a bird, he has to teach himself how, and he can only do this by writing and burning a great many bad verses. Bayard Taylor wrote poems and stories and essays which delighted him until he discovered that they were bad, when they were straightway consigned to the flames. He was passionately fond of reading, and as there were but few books in his father's house he borrowed from the neighbors when they had any to lend. There

was a library in the village containing about two hundred volumes which he read through by the time he
was thirteen.   There were some good books in this
little collection.   Gibbon, Robertson, and Sterne, and
Mrs. Hannah More; and there were elementary
scientific works, and sundry volumes of travel.   He
read for instruction more than for amusement, and
the reading most to his taste, after poetry, was that
which related to other countries and quarters of the
globe.   A set of the Penny Magazine was eagerly
devoured, especially the articles on Italy and Greece,
and those in which the lives of famous artists were
narrated.   A taste for poetry, which is the highest of
all the arts, is frequently accompanied by a taste for
art, which is poetry in its way.   It was so accompanied in the mind of Bayard Taylor, whose greatest
desire, after the desire to excell in poetry, was to be
a painter.   With this object in view he resolved
when he was sixteen to learn engraving, in the hope
of becoming a painter afterward, and made a journey
to Philadelphia, where he spent a week or two trying
to obtain a situation in an engraver's office.   But it
was not to be.   So he returned to Kennett Square
and poetry.   He had already passed six months at a
boarding-school, where he studied Latin, French and
Spanish.   He was bound to have an education some-

how. His father, who was a farmer, naturally thought that less devotion to books, and more devotion to farming, would be better for him in the end, or at any rate would be better for the farm. Most country parents thought so forty or fifty years ago, when any of their children were given to reading, which they really considered a waste of time! We know better than that now, but see what our chances are compared with the chances of our ancestors. Bayard Taylor's mother stood by him, like the motherly woman she was, and is, and his reading went on. I know this good old lady, who is now in her seventy-eighth year — his father is four years older — and know what he owed to her in his youth. But I must not write about Rebecca Taylor, nor Joseph Taylor, as they call them at Kennett Square, which is a settlement of Friends. Both were, and I believe still are, members of this peaceful sect.

Our poet and would-be painter taught a country school the next winter after his fruitless visit to Philadelphia, and devoted his spare hours to the study of languages. At the age of seventeen he went to West Chester, a pleasant town about ten miles from Kennett Square, and entered into a printing office in order to learn the trade of a compositor. It is a tedious labor which is performed mechanically, and it left him no opportunity for study, and but little for reading. Still he persisted in it for more than a year, and worked away at his Latin at night. He now began to publish poetry in the country newspapers, and when he was eighteen he had enough to make a little volume. Armed with this booklet, which opened with a narrative poem called "Ximena," he went again to Philadelphia, and saw the great Dr. Griswold, who was the editor of "Graham's Magazine," and who advised him to publish it. He did more than that — he showed his faith in the printer-poet by accepting one of his poems for his magazine. Another great man of that day, N. P. Willis, published two of his poems which had been sent to him in the "New Mirror," of which he was the editor, with a notice which made the writer of the poems jubilant. He was beginning to be recognized. A few months later, a cousin of Bayard Taylor determined to go to Germany to study at Heidelberg, and he instantly determined to go with him, and to pay his way by getting engagements as a newspaper correspondent. It was a bold idea in a country lad of nineteen, but it succeeded, for correspondents were not as plentiful thirty-three years ago as they are to-day. Money must be raised at once, and to raise it "Ximena" was published by subscription, Chester

County furnishing names enough to pay the expenses of an edition. The Philadelphia papers spoke well of the little poetical venture, which was handsome of them, but somehow they didn't seem to want a European correspondent. Finally, however, the "United States Gazette" and the "Saturday Evening Post" each agreed to take twelve letters from the young poet, and to pay the munificent price of fifty dollars for them. Dr. Griswold accepted four poems, for which he paid the enormous sum of forty dollars. Bayard Taylor went to Europe in June, 1844, with only one hundred and forty dollars, and the money lasted until the next February. He lived eight months, in a strange country, on less than eighteen dollars a month. At the end of that time the "Saturday Evening Post" sent its correspondent fifty dollars for twelve letters more, and Dr. Griswold sent his poet fifty dollars for four more poems. Poems had risen two dollars and a half each, but letters remained at the old rate of four dollars and sixteen cents and sixty-six one-hundredths of a cent each. If Bayard Taylor ever looks back to this period of his life I think he wonders at the courage he displayed then, and at the prudence which preserved him from starvation. At any rate I wonder at both.

There are events in the life of every man which

decide his calling, and this visit of Bayard Taylor to
Europe decided his calling as a traveler. After re-
maining abroad about two yeas, during which time he
mastered German, and became tolerably familiar with
Italian and French, he returned to America and to
his home in Kennett Square, when he collected and
carefully revised his letters of travel. He then decided to republish them in a volume, and went to
New York to find a publisher. That important personage was found with great difficulty, and only
on the condition that N. P. Willis would write a
preface to the volume. Mr. Willis, who was a kind-
hearted man, and noted for his generosity to young
authors, wrote the preface at once, and the book,
which was appropriately named "Views Afoot," was
published, and very warmly praised. It was a com-
mercial success, or what was considered one at the time,
for two thousand copies were sold in six months. Bayard Taylor was now twenty-one and was making a
name in literature. So far well, but until it was
made how was he to live? He could not live by
literature in Kennett Square, where not even a newspaper was printed ; nor could he obtain any situation
on any newspaper in Philadelphia. What was to be
done? He started a newspaper with a friend, who
had been one of his comrades in the printing office in
West Chester, — a weekly newspaper in Phœnixville,

Chester County. It was what an ideal newspaper may
be — neutral in politics, so of course it offended both
parties. It was probably not local enough, so the
inhabitants of Phœnixville were not interested in it.
At the end of a year its enterprising editors and publishers were twelve hundred dollars in debt. Bayard
Taylor resolved to give up his share, and leave the
place. He wrote letters to several editors and authors in New York, and they advised him to go there.
It was wise advice, as it proved in the end, though
the outlook at first was gloomy. His earliest employment was that of assistant editor on the "*Literary
World*," under a brother poet, Charles Fenno Hoff-
man, who could only afford to pay him five dollars a
week. A month or two later he obtained a situation
on "*The Tribune,*" at a salary of twelve dollars a
week. If going to Europe decided his calling as
a traveler, "*The Tribune*" decided his calling as a
writer for many years. It was the beginning of his
popularity, for it enabled him to reach a larger audience than his books had yet reached, and it was the
beginning of his prosperity. Nearly thirty years
have passed since he wrote his first editorial in
"*The Tribune,*" and he is still writing editorials in it.

When I first made Bayard Taylor's acquaintance
he had not been in New York long. He was editing
"*The Union Magazine,*" for our common friend, Mrs.

Caroline M. Kirkland, who was spending her holidays in Europe ; and some errand of my own, I forget what, took me down to the Tribune building, and up into the editorial office. It was not in the Tall Tower, which then was not, but, as I remember, on the top floor of the old brick building, where the compositors were at work. I cannot exactly place the young editor at this visit, but I think there was a railing round him and a fellow editor. My next remembrance places him at a desk on the floor below the composing room, on the south side of the room, near one of the windows that looked out on Spruce street. I don't quite know how it was, but we were soon friends. Perhaps the fact that we were nearly the same age — we were born in the same year — and that we both wrote what we thought was poetry (I am not quite so sure of it now) may have had something to do with it. It was not long before it was our custom to spend the Saturday evenings together in his room in Murray street — I think it was Murray street — where we read this so-called poetry in MS., where we criticised it, rather too mildly, I am afraid, and where the poet-editor tempted me into smoking strong cigars. Shall I ever pass such evenings again? Never till youth returns, and the bright enthusiasms of youth.

"There are no birds in last year's nests."

It is Bayard Taylor, the poet, and not Bayard Taylor the traveler, whom I wish the readers of "WIDE AWAKE" to know now, so I shall pass rapidly over his career as a traveler. His second voyage was to California just after the breaking out of the gold fever in the summer of 1849. He went there as correspondent of "*The Tribune,*" and the letters which he wrote to it were better than those of any other California correspondent. About two years later he went to Europe for the second time. When he re turned to America his countrymen wanted him to lecture, and he did so, giving ninety lectures during his first season. Then he published a volume of poems, which he had written while in the East, and which are the best Eastern poems ever written by an American; then a volume of prose describing a journey to Central Africa; then another volume of prose about the lands of the Saracen, and another about North China and Japan. I pass over the names of these books and the years in which they were published, and the countries that he traveled through at a later period, and come down to his marriage with a German lady, Marie Hansen, the daughter of Prof. P. A. Hansen, a distinguished

astronomer of Gotha, Germany. The happy pair
proceeded to Greece shortly after their marriage, and
the following year Bayard Taylor returned to America,
with his wife and an infant daughter, Miss Lilian
Taylor, a wild rose-bud of a young lady who is now
blooming among the recent girl graduates of Vassar
College. When Bayard Taylor was a bachelor it
mattered little where he lived; one place was as
good as another to a man of his roving disposition.
But now that he was a husband and a father it be-
hoved him to have a place which he could call his
home. He had long fixed his eyes on a spot of
ground upon which when a boy he built his castles in
Spain, and which he meant to buy some day, when it
was for sale, and he had money. It was as much a
dream at first as his voyage to Europe, but it became
a reality at last, as the voyage did, for it was for sale,
and he bought it, or rather it was bought for him
during his residence abroad. It lies in sight of, and
immediately opposite, the old Taylor homestead, from
which it is separated by a country road that goes
winding up hill and down vale through stretches of
beautiful scenery. The border which faces the road
is wooded with tall trees, through which you catch
glimpses of an undulating slope of pasture bordered
at the farther side with similar old forestry. It was

CEDARCROFT. — THE HOME OF BAYARD TAYLOR.

originally what the English call a croft, an enclosed
field, and as it was well sprinkled with cedars, Bayard
Taylor christened it Cedarcroft. The site that he
selected for his house was at the upper end of his
grounds, an elevation which sloped away in natural
terraces, and, in front, in a gentle declivity of lawn.
Nature made the spot for a poet's home, and a poet
made it his home. He went to Europe a poor boy, as
I have told you; now he was a prosperous gentleman.
Sixteen years of hard work were rewarded in Cedarcroft. I am not enough of an architect even to guess
what style of architecture is represented in Bayard
Taylor's house, nor indeed do I care. It is enough
for me to know that it is a large, comfortable country
house, with a fine outlook on the surrounding country,
which to my mind is the perfection of pastoral landscape. I like the seaside better than any inland
scenery, but after the seaside give me Kennett
Square from the tower at Cedarcroft.

When Cedarcroft was finished, Bayard Taylor gave
his friends and neighbors what might be called a
house-warming. I went there as his old acquaintance,
and one pleasant summer day, when the last finishing
touches were going on, he or I conceived the
idea of writing a play and producing it in the new
house before a country audience. We retired myste-

riously into a room by ourselves, in the tower, if my
memory serves me, and commenced our wonderful
labors. We set to work like another Beaumont and
Fletcher, and selected a theme. Then we remembered
the capacities of those whom we had chosen to play
when the play should be written, and fitted them
with parts ; then we began to write. Sometimes
Bayard Taylor wrote a whole scene without any
help from me ; sometimes I wrote a whole scene without any help from him ; and sometimes we wrote a whole
scene together, he the speeches of one character, I the
speeches of another, and so on. We finished the play
in two or three days, and gave the actors their parts
to learn, I filling the difficult and thankless part of
Stage Manager, as well as my own part. The library,
which was at the farther end of the house, facing the
barn, was turned into a stage by running up a
partition of muslin sufficiently far from the walls to
allow us to enter unperceived from the green-room,
which, by the way, was the dining-room, and to make
our exits and entrances properly. When our company had learned their parts, and had gone through
enough rehearsals to acquit themselves creditably,
we went to an old, disused printing office in Kennett
Square, and set up and printed bills for the per-
formance. The important day came, and the guests

came, some of them, I believe, from miles away, simple-minded country folk, many of whom had never
entered, or perhaps heard of, a play-house. The parlor, which fronted the library, and the hall between
the parlor and the library, were packed with the
audience. The bell tinkled, and the curtain rose,—
or were the library doors run into the partition wall?
I have forgotten, nor does it matter now. The play
began. The scene was a country hotel, at which two
ladies were stopping, an aunt and a niece, one of
whom was wealthy. Bayard Taylor, an army officer
on a furlough, was in love with the niece, to whom I
made love on account of her supposed wealth. I was
an airy, impudent scamp, such as are occasionally
found at hotels, living extravagantly on nothing a
year. The landlord of the hotel was a tall young
man who stuffed himself out into a Falstaff with bed
pillows. There was a Yankee servant girl, an Irish
servant man, and other characters which I have forgotten. Army officer was jealous of scamp, for making love to his girl: landlord was enraged with
scamp, for not paying his board bill: scamp was in
a quandary between niece and aunt. You can make
the play out of this to suit yourselves, and I have no
doubt but it will be as good as the one we made,
which appeared to delight our simple-minded audi-

ence, who laughed at the jokes, but missed the best joke of all, namely, that there was not one original character, situation, speech, thought or word in the whole thing! That was the joke of "Love in a Hotel," which was played, for the first and last time, one summer day seventeen years ago at Cedarcroft.

Eight years after this humorous house-warming, Cedarcroft was again the scene of festivity. Fifty years had passed since Joseph Taylor and Rebecca Way took each other for better or for worse, and their friends were invited there to celebrate their golden wedding. All their children who were in America were present, with a host of friends and neighbors. The house was overflowing with guests. A little literature was served up to them in the shape of a Masque, which was written by the master of the house, and performed by nine young ladies and one young gentleman. Among the characters were three fairies, the Fairy of Domestic Life with two attendant fays, and seven spirits, three being the cardinal virtues of Truth, Charity, and Temperance, and four impersonations of America, Africa, Switzerland and Germany ; Germany being the birthplace of Mrs. Taylor, and Switzerland the residence of one of Bayard Taylor's married sisters. It was a pretty piece of verse, and it went off well. After it was finished, two poetical greetings were read by the

Bayard Taylor.

writers thereof, one being the poet Boker, the other your humble servant. I ought to remember the the Golden Wedding better than I do, for it occurred only nine years ago, and I see it still in my mind's eye, but somehow two hundred people, young and old, in one house, are too many for me. Cedarcroft was populous that bright October day; the parlor, the library, the dining-room, swarmed with life and resounded with merriment.

I would like to describe Cedarcroft, if I knew how, but I do not; I have no talent for description. My favorite room when I am there is the library, where I see Bayard Taylor seated at his desk, translating "Faust" may be, or writing a book of travel. He is busy, but not so busy as to be entirely absorbed in his work. He can smoke and talk without losing the thread of his thought. I leave him writing in the library and pass out on the piazza, the pillars of which are draped with vines; down the terrace and past the flower-beds into the green lawn bordered with trees; down the lawn to the pond at the end; back through the belt of trees on the roadside border of Cedarcroft, and up till I strike the drive and follow it to the arched portico of the tower. Then I stroll off to the orchard, the grapery, or where I will, for Cedarcroft is but another name for Liberty Hall.

I am not going to describe Bayard Taylor to you,

nor to tell you about his books, which you have read,
or can read yourselves.   Whatever your taste may be,
you will be sure to find something in them that you will
like.   He has published, let me see, — eight volumes
of poetry, twelve volumes of travel, four volumes of
novels and stories, and translations of the two parts
of "Faust," — twenty-six volumes in less than thirty-
three years, to say nothing of the works he has edited,
his magazine papers, his lectures, and his thousands
of newspaper articles.   He loves writing, and is
never so happy as when seated at his desk bending
over the paper which he covers so calmly with his
beautiful penmanship.   Such, as I know him, is the
poet Bayard Taylor.

W. D. HOWELLS.

IN Cambridge, Massachusetts are the homes of a number of poets, and prose writers, whose names have become more or less famous throughout the world of literature and art. I think I may also say that most of these homes are grouped together, as it were, within the radius of a single square mile, thus illustrating what ought to be an old adage, that authorship likes close company.

Be that as it may, if you will take the horse-car at Bowdoin Square in Boston, and get out at Harvard Square, in Cambridge, you will find yourself very nearly in the centre of what may be termed a literary habitation. Whichever way you turn, or whatever street you may choose to follow, you are pretty sure to pass the door of a pen-worker before you have gone on many steps ; and, if you keep going onward a little ways and then swing round the circle, like somebody

119

of whom Parson Nasby used to tell, you will, by the time you arrive back at your starting place, have caught a glimpse of where Holmes and Everett, and Sparks used to live, as well as where Longfellow, and Lowell, and Howells and a host of others still live and thrive.

I dare say, when you have beheld all of these wondrous sights, — which are not so wondrous after all, when once you have thought about them, — you will ask the question, why have so many literary men chosen to make their homes in Cambridge? I have asked this question over a hundred times, and I fancy that I have not found the answer yet. Perhaps, indeed, Harvard College is the great attraction, or rather the Library which belongs to Harvard College, and which is a precious source of usefulness to a person engaged in literary research. Perhaps, again, it is the old town itself, with its splendid elms, its quaint old houses that have come down from an early day, and its countless other relics of historic times, which lends inspiration to the intellectual worker and keeps him aloof from the busy, bustling world without. And, perhaps, finally, Cambridge is no more attractive in itself than many other New England towns, and not half so stirring and so enterprising. I have dreamed at times that, if some great giant were to

RESIDENCE OF W. D. HOWELLS, CAMBRIDGE, MASS.

swallow up the venerable institution of learning to-gether with all of its traditions and associations, this famous town of Cambridge would be in reality what some of the foes without, have asserted it to be already, a sort of Sleepy Hollow, where half of the people scribble, and the other half read and admire.

But I fear you may be taking the horse-car back to Boston before I have had my say, if I do not come at once to my subject. To begin again ; if you will ac-company me, in a five minutes walk, through Harvard Square, up Garden street, pass the Common, whence the patriots of '75 started on their memorable march to Bunker Hill, and then up the beautiful Concord Avenue which winds onward and onward through sun-light and shadow until it loses itself, twelve miles away, in the first battlefield of the American Revolu-tion, I will show you the home of William D. Howells, a graceful poet and a writer of deliciously sweet Eng-lish prose.

It stands a little back from the main street, and is hemmed in on all sides by tall, noble trees which, in summer time, fairly embower it with their foliage. The house is newly built in the modern style, and, in its external appearance, does not vary materially from many other similar edifices which are visible around it. Having passed through the gate, a short

narrow path conducts you to the main entrance, which
is on the north side of the house. The bell rings;
the door opens ; and, a moment later, you sit down in
the study of the poet.

The picture which the artist has drawn will give
you a much better idea of this "study" than it is possible for me to convey in words. It is not a very
large room, nor, indeed, is it very small. On the
whole it is an agreeable compromise between bigness
and littleness, whereby is gained one of the snug-
gest, cosiest and most homelike "quarters" that a
poet could desire.

As you enter the room, the eyes first center on the
well planned fireplace, with its polished dog-irons
standing out from the hearth and its capital set of
mantel shelves, whereon are sundry pieces of old
china, enamels, Venetian work, and other knick-knacks
of story and interest. Two sides of the room are re-
served for book shelves, which, at a glance, you will
observe are pretty nearly filled. In the centre of the
room is the poet's desk, on which many of his poems,
and all of his stories, have been penned. Mr. Howells, it need hardly be said, is a very orderly personage, and I fancy that he will not chide me for saying
that almost everything finds a place in his study and
— is in its place always. There are pictures on the

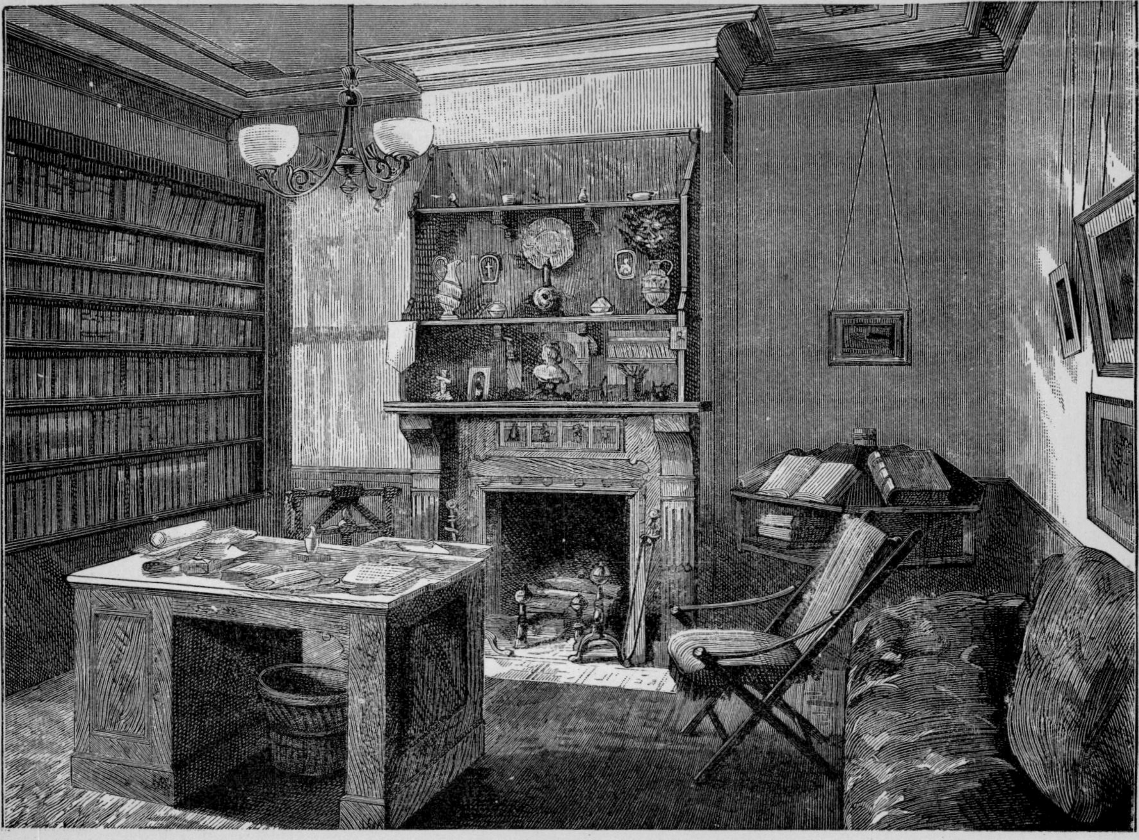

MR. HOWELLS' STUDY.

walls and pictures in portfolios, — the most attractive of these being, probably, sketches of famous men and women, whom the poet has seen and known.

One would say, after looking carefully through this room, that its busy occupant ought certainly to be among the happiest of men. Well, he is a happy and contented man, who takes the world as it goes, and rarely frets if it happens not to go as he would have it. Somebody has said that he could always read a man's biography in his portrait, and surely, whether you accept or reject this assertion it matters not, Mr. Howells' friends would agree that his likeness gives a very fair idea of the man himself.

Like most of the literary people now living in Cambridge, Mr. Howells is not a native of the place, but has been lured thither by that strange, mysterious influence of which I have already spoken in doubt. He is a Western man, born and bred to the bone ; and on the 1st of March, 1837 — just forty years ago — he first saw the light in Martinsville, Belmont Co., Ohio.

His ancestry, on the paternal side, were Welsh Quakers. In 1808, his grandfather landed in Boston, went thence to York State, where he set up woollen mills in several localities, and, finally, drifted to Ohio, where he long lived and was known as an ardent

Methodist, as well as a strong anti-slavery man. On the maternal side, his grandfather was Irish, and his grandmother a Pennsylvania German.

Mr. Howells' father was always a newspaper man, and inherited the literary taste, and ideas of thrift of his own parentage. In those early days, however, the West was not the El Dorado Land which it has since become, and those who went thither to help build it up, found much to do, with little to pay. So it was nothing very remarkable for a man to work year after year, and, at the end, to find himself no richer than when he first started.

In 1840, when the subject of my sketch was in his third year, his father left Martinsville, and removed to Hamilton, where he had previously purchased the Whig paper. It was during his nine years sojourn in this place that the future poet and novelist first manifested a liking for literary pursuits. He had already gained a fair familiarity with the writings of the English poets, and was particularly fond of the masterpieces of Sir Walter Scott. He was also an earnest student of history, and knew Greece and Rome almost by heart.

At a very early age, he does not remember exactly when, — he began to set type and to learn the printer's trade. He was somewhat skilled in this kind of work long before he could reach up to the compositor's case. While at work, he always took a just pride in what he was doing ; and before he left Hamilton, he was as much an adept in his art as was many an older workman.

During all these years, he had little or no schooling, and perhaps the best teacher he ever had was the experience he gained at the printer's desk. When the nine years had gone by, his father resolved to journey elsewhere. Sometime before this, the prosperity of his newspaper had suffered from his unstinted expression of anti-slavery opinions. He had also dared to oppose the Mexican War, which he believed had been begun and was waged without just cause ; and while clinging to these principles, he could not, of course, prove himself a very staunch supporter of General Taylor for the presidency. He had therefore sold out his newspaper, and, in 1849, removed to Dayton and became proprietor of the Dayton *Transcript*.

Hitherto this newspaper had been published as a semi-weekly. The new owner now converted it into a daily, of which the work of editing and printing was wholly performed by Mr. Howells and his three sons. The poet used to work on the paper through the day and oftentimes late into the night, and then, while an elder brother was printing the edition, he would sleep out the hours until again reminded that a new day had begun, and he must deliver the papers to the subscribers before breakfast. This was a hard school, it will seem to many; but then the discipline and the experience were invaluable.

Mr. Howells worked at the printer's trade for about ten years. But meanwhile, he stored his mind with other things. He still continued to read the works of standard authors; and, when he was moved to do so, he wrote an occasional poem, and published it in his father's newspaper.

In 1850, or thereabouts, his father being then a reporter of Legislative Proceedings for the *Ohio State Journal*, Mr. Howells also removed to Columbus, where he worked as a compositor on a salary of four dollars a week. Thenceforth till 1858, he was occupied as compositor, reporter and country journalist, and was then appointed news editor on the *State Journal*, holding the position till August, 1861.

Some time previous to this appointment, he made a trip to St. Louis by water, in company with his uncle, who was associated with one of the steamboat lines of the day. This excursion pleased him immensely, for never before had he beheld so much of the world. It revealed to him new scenes and incidents, and out of the materials thus furnished he afterwards wove that well-known poem, called the "Pilot's Story," which first appeared in the *Atlantic Monthly* in 1860, and for which he received what seemed to him to be a very large sum of money — just twenty-five dollars!

In 1860, he published in connection with Mr. John J. Piatt, a small volume entitled: "Poems of Two Friends." Most of the contents of this little book were the productions of Mr. Piatt, another poet, and at one time a fellow-worker with Mr. Howells in the printing room of the *State Journal.*

In the spring of 1860, the National Republican Convention, which met at Chicago, nominated Abraham Lincoln for the Presidency. At the time, Mr. Howells was connected with a publishing house in Columbus, and, at the request of the proprietor, he undertook to write a campaign life of the future president. He finished the work in a few weeks, and the book sold tolerably well. By way of recompense, the author received a letter of credit on several Eastern houses, and, thus equipped, he visited the East in the summer of 1860, traveling by way of the St. Lawrence river down through New England and, finally, pausing for a while in Boston.

As I have already said, he had previously sent a number of poems to the *Atlantic Monthly*, all of which had been graciously accepted by Mr. Lowell,

who was then the editor-in-chief. His reception in
Boston was most gratifying, and he there met for the
first time many of his warmest and most valued friends
He had already gained something of a reputation for
himself, by the publication of his poems, all of which
showed perfect finish and a crystal-like clearness of
thought. One of them, in particular, was much ad
mired, — probably because it was so very short and
sweet. It is called " The Mysteries," and I quote it
here entire :

> " Once on my mother's breast, a child, I crept,
>   Holding my breath,
>   There, safe and sad, lay shuddering, and wept
>   At the dark mystery of Death.
>
> " Weary and weak, and worn with all unrest,
>   Spent with the strife, —
>   O mother, let me weep upon thy breast
>   At the sad mystery of Life."

In the autumn of 1861, Mr. Howells was appointed
United States Consul at Venice. Of his life in that
beautiful Italian city, so renowned in history and
poetry, he has given us a capital account in his "Venetian Life," a volume which was first published in
London in 1865, and in New York in the following
year. In this work one gained an idea of Venice

second only to that which he would gain from an ac-
tual residence there.

During the first year of his sojourn in Venice, Mr.
Howells led a bachelor's life ; but, in 1862, he was
married at Paris to Miss Elinor G. Mead, a sister of
the sculptor, Larkin J. Mead, of Vermont, and shortly
afterward, these "two little people," (so he himself calls
them) went to housekeeping in Venice, in the Casa
Falier, a famous old palace, looking out upon the
waters of the Grand Canal.

The "gondoliers," says Mr. Howells, "used always
to point out our palace as the house in which Marino
Falier was born, and, for a long time we clung to the
hope that it might be so ; but, however pleasant it
was, we were forced, on reading up the subject a little
to relinquish our illusion, and accredit an old palace
at Santi Apostoli with the distinction we would fain
have claimed for ours. I am rather at a loss to explain how it made our lives in Casa Falier any pleas-
anter to think that a beheaded traitor had been born
in it, but we relished the superstition amazingly as
long as we could possibly believe in it. What went
far to confirm us at first in our credulity was the residence, in another part of the palace, of the Canonico
Falier, a lineal descendant of the unhappy doge.
He was a very mild-faced old priest, with a white

head, which he carried downcast, and crimson legs,
on which he moved but feebly. He owned the rooms
in which he lived, and the apartment in the front of
the palace just above our own. The rest of the house
belonged to another, for in Venice many of the palaces are divided up and sold among different pur-
chasers floor by floor, and sometimes even room by
room."

Mr. Howell's last of four years in Venice was mostly
passed under the roof of one of her most beautiful
and memorable palaces, namely the Palazzo Giustiniani. He has designated his abode there as a kind
of permanent camping out.

"When I remember," he says "the small amount
of carpeting, of furniture, and of upholstery we enjoyed, it appears to me pathetic; and yet, I am not
sure that it was not the wisest way to live. I know
that we had compensation in things not purchasable
here for money. If the furniture of the principal
bedroom was somewhat scanty, its dimensions were
unstinted : the ceiling was fifteen feet high, and was
divided into rich and heavy panels, adorned each
with a mighty rosette of carved and gilded wood, two
feet across. The parlor had not its original decora-
tions in our time, but it once had had so noble a
carved ceiling that it was found worth while to take it

PALAZZO GIUSTINIANI. THE GRAND CANAL. CASA FALIER.

down and sell it into England; and it still had two
grand Venetian mirrors, a vast and very good painting of a miracle of St. Anthony, and imitation-antique
tables and arm-chairs. The last were frolicked all
over with carven nymphs and Cupids: but they were
of such frail construction that they were not meant to
be sat in, much less to be removed from the wall
against which they stood; and more than one of our
American visitors was dismayed at having these proud
articles of furniture go to pieces upon his attempt to
use them like mere arm-chairs of ordinary life.
Scarcely less impressive or useless than these was a
monumental plaster stove, surmounted by a bust of
Æsculapius; when this was broken by accident, we
cheaply repaired the loss with a bust of Homer, which
no one could have told from the bust it replaced; and
this, and the other artistic glories of the room, made
us quite forget all possible blemishes and defects."

But it must not be imagined that Mr. Howells was
chained down by his official duties as Consul of the
United States; on the contrary, he had many an odd
moment of leisure to himself, and such moments he
wisely consumed in making short journeys to other
places of interest.

In this way, he visited Padua, Pisa, Ferrara,
Trieste, Posaquo, Como, and Mantua; and on the

8th of November, 1864, he started on the longest
road to Rome. You may read of all these experi-

W. D. HOWELLS.

ences in the author's "Italian Journeys," which was
published in 1867.

In the autumn of 1865, Mr. Howells returned
home, pausing at London only, as we have seen, to
put the manuscript of his "Venetian Life" into the

printer's hands. He did not think it worth while to go back to Ohio, but was disposed to make the city of New York his next place of residence. Having chosen literature as his profession, he at once set to work to achieve success. For a time he wrote articles for the columns of the *New York Times*, a daily newspaper ; and, a little later, he obtained a salaried position as one of the writers for *The Nation*. Whilst attending to these journalistic duties, he also found time to make another volume, — the "Italian Journeys," — out of the materials which he had gathered in his travels.

He remained about four months on the staff of the *Nation*. On New Year's day, 1866, he received an invitation from Mr. James T. Fields to become his assistant editor on the *Atlantic Monthly*. He accepted the position, and, in the following March, removed to Cambridge, Massachusetts. In July, 1871, Mr. Fields resigned, and Mr. Howells has occupied the position of editor-in-chief of the *Atlantic Monthly* ever since.

Since his return to America, Mr. Howells has published a number of books, all of them of more than ordinary interest. In 1869, appeared his hexameter poem of "No Love Lost, A Romance of Travel," happily sketching tourist life amid the fair scenery of

Venice. In 1873 was printed the collected edition
of his poems, in one volume of very small dimensions.

In 1870, he published the "Suburban Sketches,"
which presents a very amusing but singular life-like
picture of old Cambridge, and of the experiences
which may happen to one journeying thitherward in a
horse-car to Boston. This book has proven to be a
favorite with the author's neighbors and friends, and
perhaps not a few would say, if asked, that it is the
best piece of prose writing that he had ever done.

The next book was "Their Wedding Journey,"
which came out in 1871. This was the author's first
novel, (properly speaking, it is only a novelette) and
has been greatly admired on account of its sparkling
and vivacious characterization of a young married
couple who are supposed to be making the tour from
Boston to New York, by way of the Hudson to Niag-
ara, and homeward through Canada and down the
St. Lawrence.

This lively book was followed, in 1873, by "A
Chance Acquaintance," and, in 1875, by "A Fore-
gone Conclusion," — two other novels of happy character. The latest novel, " Private Theatricals," has
not yet been put into book form, but has already
been perused by a host of readers in the pages of the

Atlantic Monthly. In 1876, Mr. Howells also wrote a "Life of Rutherford B. Hayes," the Republican candidate for the Presidency.

Mr. Howells has always been a steady and diligent worker, and never allows a day to go by without turning it to some good account. Besides the works enumerated above, he has contributed many articles of interest to the pages of the *North American Review*, and delivered a course of lectures on the modern Italian Poets, before the Boston Lowell Institute. It is to be hoped that he will find time, ere long, to revise these lectures, and to put them in book form, before a wider public.

Ever since his return to this country, Mr. Howells has been regarded as one of the foremost of American writers. His sketches of travel and of life abroad, have been greatly admired, on account of their accuracy and winning style, while his stories, which are almost devoid of plot, have attracted by their rich thought, and graceful diction.

It is not generally known, however, that the author would rather wished to be looked upon as a poet, than as a writer of genial prose : and I am not sure that the fact of his writing such prose, in the past four or five years, has not a little destroyed his reputation as a writer of equally charming verse.

I might, were I so disposed, and the limits of my
article expanded, quote in this place many a pretty
poem, that the world would not willingly let die.
Most of these have a sort of serious tone about them,
while not a few are unpardonably sad. Here is one,
however, which is neither sad or serious, and which
shows the humorous side of the poet. It is entitled
" Caprice," and is as follows : —

> " She hung the cage at the window :
>   ' If he goes by,' she said,
> ' He will hear my robin singing,
>   And when he lifts his head,
> I shall be sitting here to sew,
> And he will bow to me, I know.'
>
> " The robin sang a love-sweet song,
>   The young man raised his head ;
> The maiden turned away and blushed :
>   ' I am a fool,' she said,
> And went on broidering in silk,
> A pink-eyed rabbit, white as milk.

II.

> " The young man loitered slowly
>   By the house three times that day ;
> She took her bird from the window :
>   ' He need not look this way.'
> She sat at her piano long,
> And sighed, and played a death-sad song.
>
> " But when the day was done, she said,
>   ' I wish he would come !

Remember, Mary, if he calls
    To-night — I'm not at home.'
So when he rang, she went — the elf —
She went and let him in herself.

III.

"They sang full long together
    Their songs love-sweet, death-sad :
The robin woke from his slumber,
    And sang out, clear and glad.
'Now go !' she coldly said ; ''tis late ;'
And followed him — to latch the gate.

"He took the rosebud from her hair,
    While, ' You shall not ' ! she said :
He closed her hand within his own,
    And, while her tongue forbade,
Her will was darkened in the eclipse
Of blinding love upon his lips ."

But I must have done ; and to tell the truth, there is scarcely more to tell you. The poet is but a young man yet, and we may all hope that his work is just begun. At home, he is happy, contented, genial, affable, and one of the best and brightest conversationalists. He is fond of children, and he has three of them, the eldest, Winifred, having been born at the Casa Falier in 1863. If you were to call upon him, some fine day, you would find him to be very much of a boy, and, though older indeed than most boys, possessing certainly a very young and jovial heart.

You should take care, however, not to pay your visit in working hours, that is to say, from nine o'clock in the morning, till one o'clock in the after-noon.

RICHARD HENRY DANA.

"WHOM the gods love die young," was a saying of the ancients. We moderns know that there are no gods either to love or hate, but we understand what these old idolaters meant. They simply meant that a long life was denied to the possessor of great abilities, — that the finest geniuses had the shortest lives. Was it true then? is it true now?

Let us see whether it was true of the ancient poets, and is true of the modern poets. Everybody knows that Thomas Chatterton was a wonderful genius, and that he perished young. The poor boy poisoned himself before he was eighteen. Henry Kirke White who was a pleasing poet, died before he was twenty-two, and Michael Bruce, a minor Scottish poet, died in his twenty-second year. Two great poets died at a comparatively early age, Shelley before he was thirty, and Byron shortly after he was thirty-six. Five of the British poets, then, may be said to have died young. But let us look further, and not merely at the British, but at the French, the German, and the Greek poets. Passing over Homer, of whom nothing is known (tradition says he was old and blind), we find that Euripides lived to be seventy-four, and Sophocles ninety. The German poet Klopstock lived to be seventy-nine, and Goethe eighty-three. The French poet Beranger lived to be seventy-seven, Corneille to be seventy-eight, and Voltaire eighty-four. The English poet Rogers lived to be ninety-two. Philip Freneau, an early American poet, lived to be nearly eighty-one. Mr William Cullen Bryant is now in his eighty-third year, and Mr. Richard Henry Dana in his ninetieth year. It is not true, therefore, that those "whom the gods love die young."

I am going to tell you something about Mr. Richard Dana, but not much, for there is not much to tell. If Mr. Dana himself were asked to tell the story of his life, he might quote the line which Canning puts into the mouth of his famous needy knife-grinder, "Story? Lord bless you! I have none to tell, sir."

Mr. Dana's family is an old and honorable one in New England. Dr. Griswold traces it back to a William Dana, Esq., who, he says, was Sheriff of

Middlesex in the reign of Queen Elizabeth ; but the
American Danas don't believe in this gentleman,
mythical or otherwise. The first Dana that came to

RICHARD HENRY DANA.

America was Richard Dana, who in 1640 settled in
Cambridge, Mass. A grandson of the same name,
who was the grandfather of Mr. Dana, and an eminent lawyer, was an active Whig in the troubles in
Boston before the breaking out of the Revolution.

His son, Francis Dana, was minister to Russia during the Revolution, a member of Congress, and a member of the Massachusetts Convention for adopting the national Constitution. He, too, was an eminent lawyer, for he rose to be Chief Justice of Massachusetts. He married a daughter of William Ellery, one of the signers of the Declaration of Independence for Rhode Island, who was the mother of our venerable poet. Mr. Dana's ancestors, we see, were men of repute in their day and generation, and if there is anything to be proud of in ancestry, and I am inclined to think there is sometimes, he has a right to be proud of them.

The ancients had among their games a race, the name of which escapes me, the runners in which bore lighted torches, which were handed on when they became exhausted to their more fortunate comrades. The torch which has been handed on in the Dana family is that of Law, which has descended through several generations, and which to-day is shining in the hands of Mr. Richard Henry Dana Jr., a hale young gentleman of sixty-two. If I were given to fanciful speculations, I might trace the torch of Poetry, which has long expired in the hands of Mr. Dana, back into the hands of our early poetess, but it is not worth while, for she is so obscure that I will wager a trifle — say my head — that no reader of "Wide Awake" ever heard of her, and few, if any, of their parents either. Who knows who Mistress Anne Bradstreet was, — the tenth muse springing up in America?

Mr. Richard Henry Dana, was born in Cambridge, November 15th, 1787. A delicate child, of uncertain health, unable to apply himself to constant study, he passed much of his time in rambling over the rocks at Newport, where he was taken when about ten years old, and where his mind was in unconscious sympathy with his surroundings. If the old woods and bleak hills of Cummington inspired young *Master* Bryant to write "Thanatopsis," the rocky shore and the wild waves of Newport inspired Mr. Dana to write "The Buccaneer."

But I must not let myself outrun his childhood which was an out-door one, as I have said, at any rate, until he returned to Cambridge and entered Harvard College, where he pursued his studies until his twentieth year, when he left college, and returned to Newport. So Dr. Griswold says, and adds that he spent two years in studying the Latin language and literature, — as if he had not already studied them!

This brief paragraph covers the first twenty years of Mr. Dana's life, so you see I was right in saying

that there was not much to tell.   Perhaps it will be
more interesting later on.

I have spoken of the ancestral torch of the Dana
family.   It was now committed to the hands of Mr.
Dana, and he may be said to have kindled it in the
office of his cousin, Francis Dana Channing, with
whom he studied law, and with enough success to be
admitted to the Boston bar.   He was also admitted
to the bar of Baltimore, where he resided for a time.
At the age of twenty-four he was elected to the legislature of his native State, and three years afterwards
he made his first appearance in Literature, as the
author of an oration which he delivered on the cele-
bration of the Fourth of July, which meant more to
our ancestors than it meant to us, especially at that
time, when they were wrought up with their second
war with England.   Orator, politician, lawyer — Mr.
Dana's chances of becoming a poet were not brilliant
at twenty-seven.

If I knew just how much the majority of the read-
ers of "Wide Awake" knew about the history of
American literature sixty or seventy years ago, I
should know what to tell them next ; but, as I do not,
I must proceed as well as I can.   Briefly, then,
America had no literature worth speaking of when
Mr. Dana delivered his Fourth of July oration.   One

novelist had appeared, in the person of Charles
Brockden Brown, who wrote five or six uncanny stories ; and two essayists, James K. Paulding and Washington Irving, who wrote together a series of papers
called "Salmagundi." "The Sketch Book" did not
exist, none of Cooper's novels were written, and there
were no magazines, or what we to-day would think
were magazines. A graduate of Harvard College
had commenced a monthly Anthology when Mr.
Dana was sixteen years old. It was managed by a
club of gentlemen, of whom he was one, and when
that publication expired, as it did at the end of eight
years, this club grew into another, which four years
later started the "North American Review." It had
four different editors in the first three years of its existence, the last being Mr. Edward T. Channing, who
shared his duties with his cousin Mr. Dana, whose
literary life may be said to have begun in its pages.
Nobody that I have heard of ever had a lively life on
the North American Review, and nobody, I suppose,
ever expected to.

"But you are not telling us about the life of Mr.
Dana," the impatient readers of "Wide Awake"
may say. To which I reply I am telling you all I
know. I have not told you, though, that he was married before this ; but he was, for the son of whom I

have already spoken, came into the world in the same year that the "North American Review" did. Mr. Dana's connection with this periodical lasted as long as his cousin continued its editor, and when the latter was made a professor at Harvard he left it, and in the following year began to publish, in numbers, in New York, a work entitled "The Idle Man." There was no reason why it should not succeed ; " The Sketch Book" had done so six years before, but succeed it did not, so Mr. Dana stopped with the first number of the second volume. for he was writing himself into debt. He could have afforded this, I have no doubt, for his family was wealthy — his father used to ride to court in his coach, and traveled the circuits with his body-servant, — but he concluded not to do so. It was enough to lose his work without losing his money also.

The only eminent man of letters that Mr. Dana associated with — as far as I have been able to learn, I mean, — was Mr. Bryant, whose poem of "Thanatopsis" was sent to the "North American Review," when he was a member of the club who managed it. He saw its greatness at once, and walked from Cambridge to Boston, to have a view of its remarkable author. When he reached the State House, a plain, middle-aged man, with a business-like aspect, was pointed out to him. A glance was enough; the legislator could not be the author of "Thanatopsis," and he returned without seeking an interview with him. A slight mistake of names had misled his informant. So says Dr. Griswold, who adds that Mr. Dana made the acquaintance of Mr. Bryant when he came to Cambridge to deliver his poem of "The Ages" at Harvard College. The result of this acquaintance was the contribution by Mr. Bryant of several poems to "The Idle Man." They were fine, no doubt; but they failed to quicken the stagnant circulation of that languid literary personage, whose doom was nigh.

Another result was the first poem that Mr. Dana is said to have written, "The Dying Raven," which was published four years after the death of the unfortunate "Idle Man," in "The New York Review," which was edited by Mr. Bryant, his poetical friend. I do not understand how it was that Mr. Dana published no poetry before he was thirty-eight years old, but all his biographers say so, and I suppose we must believe them. "The Dying Raven" certainly was like the work of an unpracticed hand.

The habit of writing poetry grows upon one when once formed, like other habits, good or bad, and Mr. Dana was no exception to the rule, for within two years after the appearance of "The Dying Raven" he had written poetry enough to make a volume. It was published in his fortieth year, under the simple title of " Poems," of which there were nine, the most important one being " The Buccaneer." It is a story poem, and as the readers of " Wide Awake " may like to know what the story is, I will try to state the substance of it in prose.

There was once, and of course there is now, an island nine leagues off the shore, which we will suppose to be the shore of New England, and this island was the haunt of a band of pirates, whose captain was named Matthew Lee. He was a dark, low, brawny man, with thick-set brows, gray eyes, and a mocking laugh, and his heart was as cruel as his arm was strong. Such was Matt Lee, who had made great gains by piracy, but failed to keep them long, for the waste of such men is always greater than their gain.

So he made up his mind one day to try the merchant's trade, and sell what he had left. He manned his ship, put a cargo of his spoils on board, and sailed away from the island. A storm soon rose, the sea run high, and the ship sprung a leak. They worked hard at the pumps, and, to lighten the ship, threw all the cargo overboard, and just managed to reach a port with torn spars and sails.

Lee was in a furious humor, for he had lost his

cargo, and his ship was a wreck. There was no chance of his prospering by lawful trade, so he told his men that they would go to their old work again. It was a Spanish port that he was in, and the French were fighting with the Spaniards and the English in the great Peninsular war early in the present century.

A young Spanish lady wished to leave the country, which was no longer dear to her, because her husband had fallen in battle; and Lee, who pretended to pity her, offered to take her on board his ship, which had been repaired. The poor young widow trusted in his promises, and came on board, with her servants and her wealth, and a white horse she used to ride in the life-time of her husband. The sun went down on the sea, and the shadows gathered round her home. The stars burned brightly, and she looked towards the shore, beyond the waters black in night.

"I shall never see thee more," she murmured.

Sleep, sleep, thou sad one! The moon rises, and in the shadow of the mast there is a dark man. What does he growl to himself? "It is too still to-night!" So the life of the Spanish widow was spared for that night. Matt went to sleep at last, and had a dream of her which frightened him, but did not shake his purpose to murder her. "The gold will make all whole," he said.

Another night came, and he made a sign to his men, who crept down into the cabin like shadows. Suddenly there were shrieks and fiendish yells. The servants of the widow were stabbed in their sleep. The cabin lamp shone on pale dead men, on quick, fierce eyes, on hands dripping with blood. A dash, and they forced the door of the lady's cabin, There was a long, shill, piercing scream. It ceased, and like a flash of lightning a loose-robed form with streaming hair shot by. A leap, a splash, and it was gone! Lee stood like one lost. Was it a spirit that passed him? There was no tread on the deck. Who heard any? Poor girl! And she is drowned! Did she go down into the depths? How dark they looked, and cold! When he came to himself they brought up the dead, and threw them overboard. "We must not be betrayed," said Lee. "An ass, it is said, once brayed strange words. There is a horse on board, *her* horse, and he is not to be trusted. We will throw him in the waves alive. He will swim." They threw the horse into the sea, and a shriek such as never came to mortal ears rang over the waters. He drifted away at last out of sight, but they heard his dreadful cry all night.

When morning came they washed away the blood-stains and divided the booty. They sang and swore

and gambled, they laughed and drank and fought.
One stormy night the dwellers on the island I told
you of at the beginning saw boats making for the
shore. The next day at noon the people of the town
were startled by the appearance of Lee and his men.
"Here comes Lee!" the boys shouted. "Where's
your ship, Lee?"

"It took fire by chance one night, not many leagues
from shore."

This was all they learned.

They were flush of gold, — those grim pirates.

"You didn't lose your cargo, then, Lee?"

"No, heaven prospers true men. Forsake your
evil ways, as we forsook ours and took to honest
courses."

So the godless wretch mocked them. After that
he lorded it through the island. The people dreaded
his power and his smile, and none went within his
door. None, that is, except those who had dipped
their hands in blood with him, and laughed to see the
white horse swim.

When the anniversary of the murder came round
they feasted and caroused together till near midnight.

But what means that red light on the waters? A
ship, and all on fire, — hull, yards and masts, and her
sheets are sheets of flame! They gazed on each

other in dumb amazement as she rode on, shedding
a wild and lurid light around the cove. It scared the
sea-birds from their nests; they darted and wheeled
around with despairing screams. What is that coming above the waves so ghastly white? It is a spectre
horse! He gains the sands, his ghostly sides streaming with cold blue light, and his path shining like the
wake of a ship. Now he is at Lee's door, where he
sends up a neigh which rings along the sky and jars
the shore. The revelers know the sound, and their
flushed cheeks turn pale with fear. Lee drops his
cup; his lips are stiff with fright. Sit down, Lee, it
is your banquet night!

The shadow stands with his hoofs on the door-stone
of Lee's house. His hair rises as its cold breath
chills his frame, and a voice within him bids him
mount the horse. He mounts it, and is borne with
speed and dread to the hanging steep. It stops suddenly, with its feet on the verge, where it stands like
marble. A tall ship is burning, — a mass of red-hot
spars and crackling flame. She burns up, and yet is
the same:

> " Her hot, red flame is beating all the night
> On man and horse, in their cold phosphor light."

The fearful man sat looking through this cold light
on the burning ship. What do you see, Lee?

" I look where mortal man may not,
Into the chambers of the deep.
I see the dead, long, long forgot,

I see them in their sleep.
A dreadful power is mine, which none can know,
Save him who leagues his soul with death and woe."

The low, far west is bright no more.   No sound is
heard at sea or along the shore but the cry of a passing bird.

" Now long that thick, red light has shone
On stern, dark rocks, and deep, still bay,
On man and horse that seem of stone,
So motionless are they.
But now its lurid fire less fiercely burns:
The night is going — faint, gray dawn returns.

" That spectre steed now slowly pales,
Now changes like a moonlit cloud.
That thin, cold light now slowly fails,
Which wrapt them like a shroud.
Both ship and horse are fading into air.
Lee, 'mazed, alone, — see, Lee is standing there ! "

The morning air blows on him, the waves dance
before him, and the sea-birds wheel and call ; but he
does not hear their call, nor see the waves, nor feel
the breeze.   Noon comes, and the hot sun beats upon
his head, but he heeds it not.

Night comes, the sun goes down, and the gull finds
her place on shore, but there he still stands.   Go

home, Lee, and call your revelers round you. But they have fled from the island. There was no one to meet him at his house; the chairs were empty, the fires burnt out. Everybody shunned him. Children stared after him, and ran away frightened to their homes. The crowd pointed at him and said : " There goes the evil man."

He turned and cursed man and child. Terror and madness drove him to men, and hatred of man to solitude.

The second anniversary of the murder came, and with it the burning ship, and the spectre horse, which he rode as before. The islanders, who began to pity him, asked him why he wandered so, and he said he wanted to go, but wanted to go by land, and there was no way. They urged him to go on board a sloop which they had, but he said the spectre horse would not allow him to go to sea except with him.

The third anniversary of the murder came, and with it the burning ship, which this time burned up, and settled in the waves. The spectre horse rose from where it sank :

> " He treads the waters as a solid floor :
> He's moving on.   Lee waits him at the door."

He pleads that he did not do the deed alone, but he pleads in vain.   His time has come, the spectre

horse tells him, and he must go. He mounts the
horse again, and is borne to the sea.

> "He's on the beach; he stops not there.
>   He's on the sea! Lee, quit the horse!
> Lee struggles hard—'tis mad despair!
>   'Tis vain. The spirit corse
> Holds him by fearful spell;—he cannot leap.
> Within that horrid light he rides the deep.
>
> "It lights the sea around their track—
>   The curling comb, the dark steel wave;
> There, yet, sits Lee the spectre's back—
>   Gone, gone, and none to save!
> They're seen no more; the night hath shut them in.
> May heaven have pity on thee, man of sin!
>
> "The earth hath washed away its stain,
>   The sealed-up sky is breaking forth,
> Mustering its glorious hosts again,
>   From the fair south and north.
> The climbing moon plays on the rippling sea.
> —O, whither on its waters rideth Lee?"

Such is the outline of "The Buccaneer," which
could only have been written by one familiar with the
wild and rugged coast scenery of New England, and
the ever-changing waters of the Atlantic. No poet
in America but Mr. Dana could have written it, for
no other poet in America possesses his knowledge of
and love for the sea. It grew out of his early life at
Newport, and of his years of summer residence in
his country house near Cape Ann.

His house stands on the south side of Cape Ann,

in full sight of the ocean. The lawn upon which it
stands shelves off a few rods in front of it, in a steep,
gravelly cliff, about sixty feet above a sandy beach.
The remains of an old wall covered with bushes and
low trees fringe the edge of this cliff, a wild growth,
which descends its face to the beach below. The
beach, which is nearly a perfect semi-circle, is isolated,
on the right by a projecting ledge, which runs out beyond it into the sea, and is called "Eagle Head," and
on the left by the precipitous base of a hill, which
bears the ominous name of "Shark's Mouth." The
house stands nearly south, on a line with the beach,
and is sheltered on the north by a hill covered with a
thick growth of old trees. A further shelter from the
cold winds is a high wooded island, which lies a hundred rods or so from the base of the hill, and belongs
to the estate of Mr. Dana, who has an island of his
own, as well as Matt Lee, and a horse, too, though
not such a spectral one as carried that grim old pirate
to destruction. Of course I mean the horse which all
poets are supposed to ride — Pegasus! What else
could I mean?

Mr. Dana sold a portion of the estate which he
inherited at Cambridge, and bought this place, and
built a house upon it. The grounds formerly belonged
to a ship-master, of whom there was a tradition that
he had buried doubloons somewhere about there, which

MR. DANA'S HOME ON CAPE ANN.

money-diggers have tried to find, but without success.

Mr. Dana's estate contains about a hundred acres of woods, beach, rocks, island and arable land. The trees, as I have said, grow quite down to the beach, and one may stand under their thick foliage, with flowers under feet, and throw pebbles into the ocean, as I have no doubt Mr. Dana has often done, with his grandchildren.

It is a magnificent site for the house of a poet who loves the sea as Mr. Dana does. From his windows on the right he can see the light-houses at the entrance of the harbors of Salem, Boston and Marblehead. That rocky headland to the eastward is "Norman's Woe," about which Mr. Longfellow has made a ballad. Mr. Dana, poet-like, has left his place in the somewhat wild state it was in when he purchased it. There are crows there, and hawks, and occasionally he is visited by an eagle. The little bird that he has immortalized in one of his poems is plentiful there. You know the poem, of course. No? Then I advise you to get an older reader than yourself to show it to you. Make your acquaintance with Mr. Dana through "The Little Beach Bird," and read at a later period his powerful story of "The Buccaneer." In the meantime join with me in honoring our venerable poet, and repeat with me the words of one of Dickens' characters, "Lord, keep his memory green!"

RICHARD HENRY STODDARD.

THE name of Stoddard has not hitherto made much stir in the world, in arms, arts, or letters. Its derivation is doubtful, though it is believed by the heralds to be a corruption of the French word Standard.

There is, or was some ten or fifteen years ago, a Scotch Stoddart, who published a little pamphlet on the family name, and its different branches in Scotland, especially his own branch, which he traced back through barons and earls and princes to the great Charlemagne himself! Scattered through the pamphlet were the coats-of-arms, quarterings, crests, and what nots of the Stoddards, with Latin mottoes, among others "Post Nubes Lux," which is the motto of Richard Henry Stoddard, or will be when the darkness which has beclouded his fortunes has given place to light. He is the first of his name who has achieved the slightest distinction as a writer, though Mr. Austin Allibone mentions some eight or ten who have dabbled in literature. The only one of the early Stoddards who rose to the writing of verses was Mrs. Lavinia Stoddard, who died comparatively young, and left a poem entitled " The Soul's Defiance," which possesses considerable merit, of an old-fashioned kind. Three later Stoddards have followed the pernicious example of this good dame, the Stoddard of whom we purpose to write, and who has been more or less known as a poet for upwards of thirty years, Mr. Charles Warren Stoddard, a young Californian, with the same and other intellectual weaknesses, and Mr. William O. Stoddard, poet, journalist, and, during the late war, one of the private secretaries of President Lincoln.

His poetic namesakes are a source of constant annoyance to our Stoddard, who frankly says that he can write all the bad verse which the name is capable of supporting, and who has no wish to rob his fellows of their laurels.

The family of Mr. Stoddard figures in the town records of Hingham, Mass., the town in which he was born, as early as 1638. Who the first emigrant was he has no means of knowing, and if he had, his want of curiosity would probably prevent his looking into the antecedents of his ancestors. His feeling, if he has any, may be summed up in the lines of the old poet:

> "Tis poor, and not becoming perfect gentry,
> To build their glories at their fathers' cost;
> But at their own expense of blood or virtue
> To raise them living monuments. Our birth
> Is not our own act; honor upon trust
> Our ill deeds forfeit, and the wealthy sums
> Purchased by other's fame or sweat will be
> Our stain; for we inherit nothing truly
> But what our actions make us worthy of."

Mr. Stoddard's immediate ancestors were sea-faring men, his grandfather Ichabod Stoddard having sailed from Hingham to coastwise ports for many years. He had three sons, Ichabod, Martin and Reuben, who followed the sea, which was "the wild and wandering grave" of the two last. Reuben Stoddard, the father of Richard Henry Stoddard, was a remarkable man. He determined not to grow up in ignorance, as his father had done, and his brothers were doing, but to have an education, cost what it would.

He obtained his time of his father, who according to the usage of sixty years ago had a right to it until he was twenty-one, and ran in debt for his schooling, which was practical rather than profound. He rose rapidly in his profession, and was soon master and

part owner of the brig Royal Arch. About this time
he became the master and entire owner of a gallant

R. H. STODDARD.

little craft named Sophia Gurney. Where Captain,
or maybe Mate, Stoddard met Miss Gurney the Historic Muse does not relate.

She was one of a family of at least four sons and
four daughters, and was born at Abington, Mass.,

about ten miles south of Hingham. She was re-
markably beautiful, and tolerably ignorant. Her
father, Thomas Gurney, was a man who had seen
better days at one time or another, but eight strap-
ping children, with scriptural and sylvan names, by
his first wife, and three more by his second wife, pre-
vented his rising in the world. He was poor, but so
respectable that he was called Deacon ; if he had a
weakness it was for swapping horses, and he managed
it so that he always got a little money by the exchange,
and generally got a worse horse. He would have
swapped steeds with the Spectre Horseman if his
" ter boot " had been satisfactory.

Reuben Stoddard met Sophia Gurney, loved her,
married her, and went away on voyages in the Royal
Arch.

Three children were born to them, a son Charles
and a daughter Mary, both of whom died in infancy,
and a second son, Richard Henry.

About fifty years ago, while all his children were
alive, Captain Stoddard went on board the Royal
Arch, and, the crew making sail and weighing anchor,
he started for New York. He remained there several
days, and, weighing anchor once more, sailed away for
the port of Gottenburg, Sweden.

Weeks, months elapsed, and no tidings of the Royal

Arch reached the owners. She was not spoken at sea; no vessel passed her; she was never more heard of! A boat that was thought to be hers was picked up somewhere, but no timber from her was ever washed ashore. It was winter at the time, and the supposition was that she encountered an iceberg at night, and was sunk by the toppling mass. However this may have been, Captain Stoddard's young wife was left a widow, with three little children to take care of.

She was ill, but she rose from her bed, like the resolute woman she was, and began her life of widowhood. It was a tragic one, for two of her children died, and by some hocus pocus, which she never understood, she was cheated out of her dead husband's share of the "fatal and perfidious bark" in which he was lost. Her father was too poor to help her, for swapping horses was not a very remunerative pursuit, but she found a home in the house of her husband's father, where she devoted herself to the education of her boy, who never remembered learning to read, though writing gave him a great deal of trouble.

The recollections of a child are seldom so separable from each other that they can be arranged chronologically. Mr. Stoddard's earliest recollections place him in the first storey of his grandfather's house in Hingham, — a boy of five or six, now learning the hymns of Dr. Watts, and now reciting the hymn beginning:

"The day is past and gone."

This picture gives place to a high-backed pew in Dr. Richardson's church, as it was then called, which stood on a hill opposite the Stoddard house. This hill was separated from the lower end of the town by a little inlet or "wash" of the sea, and had been the burying-ground of Hingham time out of mind. The church was one of the oldest in New England.

The fatherless boy was so delicate that his life was despaired of. He was considered clever, — a show-child, who was expected to speak a piece when called upon, and who was pointed out among the towns-people as "Reuben s boy." His uncles were kind to him, and his grandfather was fond of him. As a great treat he was once allowed to accompany his grandfather to Cohasset, where a hotel was being built, and, as a greater treat, he was allowed to go to Boston with him in his schooner.

Widow Stoddard was of a roving, restless disposition, and the slightest thing was sufficient to make her change her residence. Her relatives, who were as poor as herself, moved nomadically from factory town to factory town, and she frequently accompanied them with her boy, who still has kaleidoscopic glimpses of Taunton, Valley Falls and Providence, — glimpses of factory interiors, of carding-rooms, spinning-rooms, weaving-rooms, and mule-rooms, — the slipping of leather bands over revolving wheels, the whizzing of spindles, — clatter, clatter, clatter.

Mixed with these are glimpses of Scituate, Bridgewater, Braintree and Abington. He remembers to have spent two summers and at least one winter at Abington, where he went to school for the first time, and where the towns-people were frightened by a transit of Venus, or Mercury, or some other astronomical occurrence, which they thought portended the End of the World!

At last his mother went to Boston with him, and opened a little shop at the foot of Hanover Street, near the ship-yards, which were convenient for the gathering of chips. He was sick one whole winter with the rheumatism, and so helpless that he had to be lifted in and out of bed. His mother maintained herself and him — that is, she kept body and soul together in both — by making "slop-work" for the Jews, who supplied sailors with clothing at exorbitant rates. The poor woman used to sit up and work all night, and morning used to find her asleep in her chair.

By and by Widow Stoddard made the acquaintance

of a sea-faring-man of about her own age, thirty-two, and, to better her condition and that of her son, she married him. "Reuben's boy" had another father. He was a kind-hearted, well-meaning man, without the art of getting on in the world, and such he continued to the day of his death, some thirty-six years later. He worked awhile in Boston as a stevedore, and then migrated to Providence, where a railroad was being made.

His family followed him as far as Seakonk, where the re-fathered boy went to work in a cotton factory. His step-father paid a visit to his relatives in New York, and the brilliant prospects which were held out to him determined him to remove thither. He brought his household stuff to Providence one autumn day, and shipped it on board a packet, and, with the hostages he had accepted of fortune — a wife in her thirties, and a boy in his eleventh year, — sailed for the city of his nativity, which he reached after a stormy passage of two days.

They landed at or near the Battery of a Sunday morning, and wandered up Broadway, which was swarming with hogs. There was not much to choose between the relatives of his mother and the relatives of his step-father, for they were poor on both sides, so the boy was not benefited by his change of residence.

His early recollections of New York are not over and above pleasant, for they connect themselves with his stepfather's family, who were just the people not to know, and who were the cause of his being sent into the street to sell matches. He has some pleasant memories of this period, however, for the great fire of 1835 occurred, and he was taken to see the smoking ruins; and, the circumstances of the family mending, he was sent for a time to a pay school, where the reading-book was Weems's Life of Marion. Who that has once read has ever forgotten the thrilling episode of the brave partisan leader offering the British officer a meal of roasted sweet potatoes? It was the great Weems who invented it, — the immortal Weems, who forged the little hatchet with which Washington cut down his father's cherry-tree! Who says that America has no poet?

Reading about Marion and Serjeant Jasper, and the rule of three and fractions, were the chief branches of education taught in this school, the master of which may have been a patriot, though he was certainly not an arithmetician, for he had to "fish" the answers to sums out of a Key!

From this academy of polite learning the boy was sent to a public school, where he learned nothing, though he got his lessons by heart. He had the reputation of being a clever boy, why, he knew not. He was a fluent reader, it is true, but he was no grammarian, and no arithmetician; he had no talent for writing compositions, and was incapable of speaking pieces, though he was compelled to do so.

The relation between parents and children was more exacting forty years ago than it is now; and children were taught to consider themselves nobodies, when the will of their parents was in question. Their time was not their own until they were twenty-one. Having the law, so to speak, on her side, and being herself a thrifty, hard-working woman, the mother of "Reuben's boy" resolved, when he was about fifteen, that he was old enough to earn money.

The morning papers were diligently searched, and the columns devoted to "wants" were studied and discussed. Two lawyers were finally found who wanted a boy, and the future poet was installed in their offices. His salary was small — less than a dollar a week, — but small as it was his mother allowed him fifty cents a month out of it, which large sum was thoughtfully invested in books. He haunted old book-stalls after office hours, and picked up bargains in the shape of odd volumes, mostly of the English poets. Among other poets whose acquaintance he made at this time were Beattie and Falconer. He read the story of Edwin, who was no vulgar minstrel boy, but he could not read the story of Palamon. He could see that Beattie had some claim to be considered a poet, but he could not see, nor has he ever been able to see, what shadow of a claim Falconer had.

The law transacted in these offices was mostly imaginary, so the young quill-driver had leisure to read poetry, and to write it, too. It was wretched stuff, of course, but he tried to have it printed in " The New World," a great weekly newspaper, edited by Park Benjamin, who somehow didn't see the genius of his would-be contributor, who sighed to himself, in the words of Beattie :

" O, who can tell how hard it is to climb
The steep where Fame's proud temple shines afar."

He resolved that he would succeed, however, and as a poet ; and in order to do this he would, if necessary, win a reputation first as a writer of prose ; he would make himself a novelist, like Dickens, whose " Master Humphrey's clock " he read every Saturday in " The New World." What would youth be without its ignorance and its aspiration ?

The brace of legal gentlemen whose clientless offices were tenanted by our young poet advised him to study the law as a profession, but his modesty led him to think that he lacked the capacity to do so, though he would admit the lack of no other capacity whatever! Was he not that man of men, a poet? He saw a live author in the perlieus of Themis, and procured a specimen of his penmanship. It was the novelist Ingraham, whose " Dancing Feather " he had read with delight, and who was a little remiss with his tailor.

He was a bright, pleasant gentleman, and his little lawyer's note was long treasured up. From law, for which he had no inclination, our dreamer passed to journalism. That is to say, he became a sort of factotum in the office of a new and shortlived journal which reported the sayings and doings of Dickens, who was then traveling in this country. This distant connection with authorship brought him in contact with another author, in the person of Mr. Lewis Gaylord Clarke, the editor of " The Knickerbocker Magazine," who was a contributor to the journal in question. It was soon moribund, and another situation had to be obtained.

One was found, or made. It was in a tailor's shop, where the aspiring rhymster cooled his natural ardor by sponging cloth, and encouraged his propensity for commerce by selling slop clothes to sailors. He was next installed as book-keeper in a bankrupt brush and bellows factory. From this he was transplanted to an occupation for which he was most unfit in that it demanded what he never posessed — physical strength and endurance.

What his mother was thinking of when she sent him to learn the trade of a blacksmith, he never knew; but send him she did, and he tried to learn the trade, but without success. He was put at once at the anvil, and before the day was over his right hand was so blistered that he had to open its fingers with his left hand, and detach them from the handle of the sledge hammer that he wielded.

Clearly he was not intended for a blacksmith. Even his mother saw that at the end of three or four days, and allowed him to find lighter employment. It came to him, he never quite knew how, in the shape of iron moulding, which he was apprenticed to learn, and which he did learn from his eighteenth to his twenty-first year.

It was hard work for a delicate boy, but it had to be done, for his family was poor, and idleness was discouraged. He had one consolation which could not be taken from him; the day would end, night would come, and he could write poetry. It was sorry stuff, and no one knew it better than he, but it gave him pleasure, and offended no one. He never offered it for publication, he was not vain enough for that;

but when it had served its turn and he was beyond it, he wisely committed it to the flames. Such was the life of Richard Henry Stoddard down to his twenty-second year.

Just about the time when the first Stoddard or Stoddards emigrated to New England, four brothers named Barstow concluded to do the same. They were of a good family in the West Riding of Yorkshire, a family that figured in other counties in England under their original name of Burstow, one of them, a certain Robert de Burstowe, having grants made to him in the reign of Edward the Second. The Barstows came to America, as most Englishmen of their period did, in order to better their fortunes. They settled in Massachusetts, at Cambridge, Watertown and Dedham, and pursued their avocations there and elsewhere. We find them as early as 1660 in Hanover, engaged in ship-building on the North River, a little stream which separates Hanover and Scituate from Pembroke and Marshfield. Before many years were over they were settled in Mattapoisett, a seaside town in the same county as Hingham, looking out on the Elizabeth Islands.

Here they lived, fathers and sons, and built ships for the whalers of New Bedford, and schooners and sloops for the West India and coastwise traders, —

lived, and grew rich and died, and left others of the name to succeed them and carry on their business.

MRS. R. H. STODDARD.

Here lived and died two Gideon Barstows, the last of whom had a son named Wilson, who married Miss Betsey Drew in his twenty-third year, two or three years before Captain Reuben Stoddard married Miss Sophia Gurney.

The Barstows were a prolific family, the great

grand-father of Wilson Barstow adding twenty-one
children to the population of his county, and Wilson Barstow himself was no exception to the rule.
He had nine children, of whom his second daughter,
Elizabeth, is the sole survivor.   She was born about
two years before Richard Henry Stoddard, and that
their paths would ever cross each other was the most
unlikely thing in the world.   They had no possession
in common, except such as was attached to the sea
through their fathers, and that was of the most unsub-
stantial kind.   One was drifting

"Where dreadful waves were whirled
About the roots of the world,"

the other was alive and well, and as surely a prosperous gentleman as the Thane of Cawdor was.

Elizabeth Barstow was one of those irrepressible
girls who are sometimes born in staid Puritan families, to puzzle their parents, and to be misunderstood.
Her spirits were high, and her disposition wilful.   She
had a passion for reading, but a great disinclination
for study.   Her inferiors shot past her at school, and
she was pronounced a dunce.   She was sent to the
best educational establishments in New England, including the Wheaton Female Seminary at Norton, but
she might as well have remained at home and rocked
her brothers and sisters, who arrived pretty regularly
at intervals of about two years.

The despair of her beautiful mother, who could not help being amused by her vagaries, she was the pride of her good-natured father, who was the magnate of the town and looked up to by his neighbors. She was not approved of by her schoolmates, for she would not learn ; besides she was very handsome. They could not imagine what men could see to admire in her.

She had one friend, however, a notable man in his way, though he was only the minister of Mattapoisett, where he was considered a queer old fellow. This was the Rev. Thomas Robbins, who was known to antiquarians as the author of a " Historical Survey of the First Planters of New England," and of several sermons preached on special occasions. He took a fancy to Miss Barstow when she was a child, and gave her the range of his library, which was a large one for a country minister to have, and which consisted chiefly of the classic works of the last century.

She read Addison, Steele and Dr. Johnson, — the Tattler, the Spectator, and the Rambler ; the delectable writings of Fielding, Richardson, Smollett and Sterne, —Tristram Shandy, Peregrine Pickle, Pamela and Tom Jones. She read Sully's Memoirs and the comedies of Sheridan ; if the comedies of Vanburgh and Congreve were there (but it is to be hoped not) she read those, too. She read hundreds, thousands of volumes in the good doctor's library which was to her a liberal education, and, indeed, the only education she ever had.

Such was the life of Elizabeth Barstow until her sixteenth birthday, or thereabout, when she saw her first live author. It was Mr. William Gilmore Simms, of South Carolina, poet and novelist, who was being lionized at Great Barrington, and whom she was to know years afterwards. He was a shadowy link between her and the foundry poet, if she had only known it, for he wrote his poem of "Atalantas" in Hingham, when "Reuben's boy" was about seven years old.

Hingham was also the residence of another American poet in the childhood of this boy, a Miss Frances Locke, who lives in our poetical annals as Mrs. Frances Sargent Osgood.

Mr. Stoddard had no consolation for the hardships of his foundry life except in writing poetry, or what he thought was poetry. He had one virtue not usually possessed by young versifiers, — he was in no hurry to see himself in print. He filled a good many little volumes with his metrical effusions, of which no more than one was ever extant at the same time, for

as fast as he completed one he destroyed its prede-
cessor. Finally he wrote something which seemed
not too bad to print, and printed it was in a weekly
magazine edited by Seba Smith, who was then in
vogue as the author of Major Jack Downing's Letters.
About this time he made the acquaintance of the Rev.
Ralph Hoyt, a minor American poet, who conde-
scended to read his manuscripts, and contrived to
disgust him with them and with himself. This acquaintance somehow led to his knowing Mr. Park
Benjamin, whose great newspaper he used to read
when a boy in the lawyer's offices, and who treated
him as an equal.

He sent one of his little manuscript volumes of
verse to N. P. Willis, the poet, who was editing the
"Home Journal," and he was kind enough to look
over it, and to express his opinion of it.

"I should think that the writer of this" (he wrote
in substance) "had genius enough to make a reputation. Pruning, trimming and condensing is necessary
to make it what it should be, as the same labor was
necessary to Byron's genius, and to Moore's. It is
hard work to do, and ill-paid when done."

The good opinion of Mr. Willis encouraged the
foundry poet to do better work than he had yet done.
He was further encouraged about this time by Mr.

Lewis Gaylord Clarke, a genial, whole-souled man,
who was anxious to bring forward young writers in
"The Knickerbocker," and not at all anxious to pay
them. It was impecunious to all but the editor, who
had to live, even if his geniuses starved.

A wiser and better acquaintance was next made,
and with a notable writer and an excellent woman, Mrs.
Caroline M. Kirkland. She was interested in the
worker in iron, and as she was editing a magazine at
the time she published some of his poems in it. He
was a proud man when he at last earned ten dollars
by his genius, but a good deal of a donkey, for he at
once invested it in an accordeon for a young person
with whom he was infatuated.

His first literary acquaintance of his own age was
Mr. Bayard Taylor, who had made his first trip to
Europe, and had published an account of it in "Views
Afoot," and who was one of the editors of "The
Tribune." The acquaintance soon ripened into
friendship, as Mr. Stoddard has told the readers of
"Wide Awake" in his paper on the home of Mr.
Taylor.

What with writing in Mrs. Kirkland's magazine,
"The Knickerbocker," and other periodicals, the
simple-minded purchaser of accordeons saved up
enough money to do another foolish thing, namely:
to publish a little volume of his own verses.

He called them " Footprints." They were pleasantly noticed in two or three magazines; one copy was sold; the edition was committed to the flames, and there the matter ended. The foot of the young poet left no print on the sands of time, but many weary prints on the wet sands of the hated foundry. The publication of his little volume, failure though it was, made him somewhat known among literary people. It introduced him to the notice of the great Dr. Rufus Griswold, who sat like another Apollo on the summit of Parnassus, and dispensed crowns to the poets of America,

> "Who wept with delight when he gave them a smile,
> And trembled with fear at his frown."

He put the author of " Footprints " in a new edition of his "Poets of America," and told the little story of his life, more beautifully than I could ever hope to, complimenting him on a quality which he never possessed, "indomitable energy," and on the impossible art of moulding his thoughts into the symmetry of verse, while he moulded the molten metal into shapes of grace. He was a fine writer, was Dr. Griswold, and a judicious critic, but a knowledge of foundries was not one of his strong points. He meant well, however, and was friendly to the young man, whom he introduced to the Mrs. Leo Hunter of the period, a young unmarried lady of Celtic and

American extraction, who wrote poetry and gave literary reunions. There he became acquainted with an elderly young woman who was somehow a friend of Miss Elizabeth Barstow, of Mattapoisett, Mass., whom he ought to know. He bowed, no doubt, at the distinction in store for him, for was it not a distinction for the son of a sailor to know the daughter of a ship-builder?

They finally met one summer evening at the house of the elderly young person, but nothing remarkable happened. It never does when it is expected to, and when match-making minds try to lead up to it. Mr. Stoddard and Miss Barstow were not apparently suited to each other. He was a penniless young man of twenty-five, good-looking, it was thought, with a knack at writing verses, but ill-dressed, careless in his personal appearance, and with no manners to speak of. She was a young woman of about the same age, was handsome, though a little faded, had a sharp tongue and off-hand ways, a determination of her own, and had been accustomed to be tenderly cared for all her life. The only thing they shared in common was love of books.

The young lady invited the young singer to her father's house at Mattapoisett, to spend the Fourth of July. They read and talked and walked and rode together, and very odd riding it was on his part, for he had not been on the back of a horse since he was a boy in Abington. The something that was expected to happen before happened now, neither quite knew how. He thought that he had lost his heart, as the saying is : she knew that she had not lost hers, but she rather liked him, if only for his simplicity.

To cut the matter short, for courtship is a flat affair, outside of novels, they made up such minds as they had that they might possibly do worse than to marry each other.

So they went off together one December morning, in New York, and wandered into a fold, the shepherd of which consented to unite these lost lambs. In other words, they went to the Church of the Good Shepherd, the pastor of which was the Rev. Ralph Hoyt, who found it easier to marry the poet than to praise his verses.

I don't know how the young husband and wife felt when they were made one, but I know what the old dramatist Middleton wrote about the feelings of a husband, and I hope his beautiful lines reflect the feelings of the Stoddards at this and all later times. Here they are.

"How near am I now to a happiness
  That earth exceeds not ! not another like it.

The treasures of the deep are not so precious
As are the concealed comforts of a man
Locked up in woman's love. I scent the air
Of blessings when I come but near the house.
What a delicious breath marriage sends forth !
The violet bed's not sweeter."

Before Mr. Stoddard had married he had become
acquainted with that incomparable writer, Nathaniel
Hawthorne. He met him in his own house at Concord with a party of friends, one of whom had come
to talk with him about his old college chum, Franklin
Pierce, who was a candidate for the Presidency, and
whose Life he was to write. Mr. Pierce was elected,
and it seemed to Mr. Hawthorne that a young poet
who had married on nothing a year might like a situation in the New York Custom House, so he obtained one for him.

He entered upon his official life the day before he
completed his twenty-eighth year, and he continued in
it for nearly seventeen years, devoting the best part
of his life to a thankless government. He had
charge of a room full of the strangest codgers alive ;
men fit for no other duties than he found or made for
them, and, indeed, most frequently unfit for those.
They were old, and lame, and they were incapable.
Most of them had seen better days; some of them
had been rich, and one or two had been millionaires.

Of this motley multitude he was the guide, philoso-
pher and friend, — the commander-in-chief of a very

MASTER LORIMER STODDARD.

awkward squad. But he made one friend, a young
gentleman whose friendship he still retains.

Being married, as I have said, he set resolutely to
to work to learn the only trade for which he seemed
fitted — literature. He couldn't hope to live by writing

poetry, so he taught himself to write prose, and found that he was either a slow teacher, or a slow scholar, probably both.

The habit of writing is sometimes catching, as his wife finally discovered when she caught herself penning little essays, and poems, and stories, which she brought to her husband in fear and trembling. She had a fine intellect, but it was untrained, and all that he could do for her was to show her how to train it. She was not cursed with mediocrity, but had the misfortune to be original. Her growth was slow but sure. She produced with labor, but what she produced was worth the labor, and to-day she is the best writer of blank verse of any woman in America.

Early one June morning, in the third year of their married life, the Stoddards found that a man-child had been sent to them. They thought him the most beautiful boy that ever lived, and were not alone in thinking him so. His face was as lovely as the face of one of Raphael's angels; his hair was like sunshine, and his eyes — there never were such heavenly eyes before. The unfathomable blue of the summer sky was shallow and pale beside them. And the child was as good as he was beautiful. When he was in his second summer he was taken down to Mattapoisett by his mother and his nurse, and his father tried to console himself during his absence by writing a poem about a little picture which had been taken of him.

Few poets' children have been more lovingly hymned than little Willy Stoddard (he was named Wilson, after a favorite brother of his mother's), unless it was poor Hartley Coleridge in the frosty midnight musings of his erratic father.

"I take his picture from my knee," sang the father of little Willy Stoddard, one hot summer night in New York, after he had been thinking of him and the country house to which he had gone:

> " I take his picture from my knee
> And press it to my lips again;
> I see an hundred in my brain,
> And all of him, and dear to me.
>
> " He nestles in his nurse's arms,
> His young eyes winking in the light;
> I hear his sudden shriek at night,
> Startled in dreams by vague alarms.
>
> " We walk the floor, and hush his moan;
> Again he sleeps; we kiss his brow;
> I toss him on my shoulder now,
> His Majesty is on his throne!
>
> " His kingly clutch is in my hair;
> He sees a rival in the glass;

It stares and passes as we pass ;
　　It fades.　I breathe the country air :

"I see a cottage leagues from here ;
A garden near ; some orchard trees ;
A leafy glimpse of creeping seas ;
　　And in the cottage something dear :

"A square of sunlight on the floor,
Blocked from the window ; in the square
A happy child with heavenly hair,
　　To whom the world is more and more.

"He sees the blue fly beat the pane,
Buzzing away the noontide hours ;
The terrace grass, the scattered flowers,
　　The beetles, and the beads of rain.

"He sees the gravelled walks below,
The narrow arbor draped with vines ;
The light that like an emerald shines,
　　The small bird hopping to and fro.

"He drinks their linked beauty in ;
They fill his thoughts with silent joy,
But now he spies a late-dropped toy,
　　And all his noisy pranks begin.

"They bear him to an upper room,
When comes the eve ; he hums for me,
Like some voluptuous drowsy bee,
　　That shuts his wings in honied gloom.

"I see a shadow in a chair;
I see a shadowy cradle go ;
I hear a ditty, soft and low ;
 The mother and the child are there !

"At length the balm of sleep is shed ;
One bed contains my bud and flower;
They sleep, and dream, and hour by hour
 Goes by, while angels watch the bed.

"Sleep on, and dream, ye blessed pair !
My prayers shall guard ye night and day;
Ye guard me so, ye make me pray,
 Ye make my happy life a prayer ! "

Just before Willy Stoddard was four years old there came to keep him company in the flowery garden of childhood, a little brother, with the same hair and eyes as his own. He came on earth, however, only to leave it after a few months' life. His father embalmed his innocent memory in two little stanzas :

"I am followed by a spirit,
 In my sorrow, and my mirth;
'Tis the spirit of an infant,
 Dying almost at its birth,
Unlamented, but how dear,
Since unseen, I know 'tis near !

"Would, if only for a moment,
 As I feel it, I could see.

In the light of heavenly beauty,
    Sitting on its father's knee !
It would dry this hopeless tear,
    Dropping now, it is so near ! ''

The Stoddards pursued the even tenor of their
way, he attending to his daily duties in the Custom
House, and now and then writing a lyric, just to keep
his hand in, and she attending to her duties as wife
and mother, and carefully cultivating her mind. Her
powers struck deeper and shot higher, and her stories
of New England life and character were marked by
keen insight and strange dramatic power. No other
American woman could have written them, for their
like was never written before, and has never been
written since, except by herself. The index to " Harper's Magazine " will tell you their names, and where
to look for them.

The ninth anniversary of the marriage of the Stoddards came and went, and they looked forward, if not
to happy days, which nobody could expect then, —
for war had broken out between the North and South,
— at least to a continuance of temperate happiness.
Six or seven years before, when Mr. Stoddard was
writing the small poems that he published under the
title of " Songs of Summer," he wrote from an imaginary sorrow a little poem which he called "The
Shadow." Here is the first stanza :

> " There is but one great sorrow,
>   All over the wide, wide world ;
>   But that in turn must come to all —
>   The Shadow that moves behind the pall,
>   A flag that never is furled ! "

The great sorrow of his life came to him in December, 1861. His little boy Willy, who was in his seventh year, was taken ill on a Monday morning. On Tuesday morning his father went down to the Custom House in order to get excused for the day, on account of his illness. He reached home early in the forenoon and found the boy — dead. A thunderbolt dropped out of heaven at his feet could not have startled him more than this sudden taking off of his beautiful one. There was nothing serious in mortality to him from that fatal day — nothing! For, as he had sung ignorantly in "The Shadow," how ignorantly ! —

> " 'Tis a blow that we never recover,
>   A wound that never will heal ! "

His friend Launt Thompson, who had made a medallion of the lad the previous summer, came to the house that night and took a cast of his little dead hand. That cast, the medallion, and a lock of curly golden hair, are all that remind him that his son Willy ever lived ; only these, and a sorrowful but immortal memory.   What was *he* was taken to Mattapoisett and interred in an old burying-ground there.

His death nearly killed his mother, and if the hearts of men *could* break *would* have broken the heart of his father, who, at a later period, celebrated his glorious little life and sudden death in the saddest verses that he ever wrote ; verses much too sad for the young readers of " Wide Awake " to see.

One December forenoon, not quite two years later, Mr. Stoddard, who was excused as before for the day, sat down at his table and wrote a little poem about a bird which had flown to his humble house.

THE BIRD.

" Out of the deeps of heaven
    A bird has flown to my door,
As twice, in the ripening summers,
    Its mates have flown before.

" Why it has flown to my dwelling,
    Not it nor I may know ;
And only the silent angels
    Can tell when it shall go !

" That it will not straightway vanish,
    But fold its wings with me,
And sing in the greenest branches
    Till the axe is laid to the tree,

" Is the prayer of my love and terror,
    For my soul is sore distrest,

> Lest I wake some dreadful morning,
> And find but its empty nest."

When I mentioned Mrs. Stoddard's poems and stories I should have spoken of her novels, "The Morgesons," "Two Men," and "Temple House." They are the most original and most powerful novels ever written by an American woman, and, like her shorter stories, grip hold of the stern, hard realities of New England life. She has no superior, unless it be Hawthorne, as a student of character, and as a delineator of live men and women. She can be humorous, and she can be pathetic. She is thought to have more of the quality called genius than her husband, who certainly has more talent than she.

His poetry is his best work, but one cannot live by poetry, which must be to most poets its own exceeding great reward. He taught himself to write prose, and produced two little books for children, "Adventures in Fairyland," and "Town and Country." The children of twenty years ago liked them, though he could never bring himself to do so. He wrote a "Life of Humboldt," for which he wonders at himself now, and he edited a series of "Bric-a-brac" books, which everybody thought good. He has contributed to all the magazines in the country, including "Wide

Awake, and to more newspapers than he can remember, and on all subjects, except theology and politics.

I have said nothing so far of the little bird that flew to his door one December forenoon, fourteen years ago. He has not flown, like his brother Willy, and his nameless little brother, who died so young, but is as live a bird to-day as any that ever twittered from the summer boughs. He is thought to be a clever lad, is Master Lorimer Stoddard, though he has the good sense not to think so himself. He is tall for his age, slight of build, addicted to reading everything except poetry, for which he cares nothing, greatly to the joy of his father, who thinks that there are altogether too many poets now, especially Stoddards. If he has any talent, after that of trying to have his own way all the time, it is probably for painting. His father knows that there are too many painters, and hopes that he will never be one. His mother called him "Lolly Dinks" when he was young, and wrote an amusing little book about him, and his odd fancies and doings.

As I have given you a glimpse of Willy Stoddard, as his father saw him in his thoughts, in his second summer at Mattapoisett, it is only fair to Lorry Stoddard to give you a glimpse of him, and his father and mother, in their home in New York.

Here is what he was to his father four years ago :

THE FOLLOWER.

" We have a youngster in the house,
    A little man of ten ;
Who dearest to his mother is
    Of all God's little men.
In-doors and out he clings to her,
    He follows up and down ;
He steals his slender hand in hers,
    He plucks her by the gown.
' Why do you cling to me so, child ?
    You track me everywhere ;
You never let me be alone.'
    And he, with serious air,
Answered, as closer still he drew,
' My feet were made to follow you.'

" Two years before the boy was born,
    Another child, of seven,
Whom Heaven had lent to us awhile,
    Went back again to Heaven.
He came to fill his brother's place,
    And bless our failing years ;
The good God sent him down in love,
    To dry our useless tears.
I think so, mother, for I hear
    In what the child has said
A meaning that he knows not of,
    A message from the dead.
He answered wiser than he knew,
' My feet were made to follow you.'

" Come here, my child, and sit with me,
    Your head upon my breast ;
You are the last of all my sons,
    And you must be the best.

How much I love you, you may guess
    When, grown a man like me,
You sit as I am sitting now,
    Your child upon your knee.
Think of me then, and what I said
    (And practiced when I could),
'Tis something to be great and wise,
    'Tis better to be good.
O, say to all things good and true,
' My feet were made to follow you.'

"Come here, my wife, and sit by me,
    And place your hand in mine
(And yours, my child), while I have you
    'Tis wicked to repine.
We've had our share of sorrows, dear,
    We've had our graves to fill;
But, thank the good God overhead,
    We have each other still!
We've nothing in the world beside,
    For we are only three;
Mother and child, *my* wife and child,
    How dear you are to me!
I know — indeed, I always knew,
My feet were made to follow you!"

The Stoddards live in New York, as I have said, in an unpretending little house in East Fifteenth Street. If I should attempt to characterize their home in a few words, I should say that it was nearly such a home as all authors ought to have. It is plainly furnished, but is full of good books, and good pictures most of which were painted by their artist friends. The books are all English, of course, for the Stod-

MR. STODDARD'S LIBRARY.

A. Lewin del. 1877. No. 1

Publb.Tucker N.Y.

dards have only such education as they have given themselves; but they are all good, "books which are books," as Charles Lamb used to say.

You see what the library looks like in the spirited drawing which Mr. Alexander Laurie has made of it, though you miss the color in the rooms, — in the Turkey rug on the floor, in the pictures on the walls, and in the china vases and the like on the mantel and the writing-desk.

There is another room over the library which is full of books and engravings. Mr. Stoddard keeps there his collection of English poetry, new and old, which is an excellent one, his friends say when they consult it, as Mr. Stedman did when he was writing his "Victorian Poets." He keeps his autographs there also, and his books which once belonged to great men. He could show you, if he would, the books of Byron, Coleridge, Wordsworth, Southey, Lamb, Leigh Hunt, Campbell, Gray, Pope, Sterne, Churchill, and many more famous English poets; and he could show you, if he would, a mahogany box full of manuscripts from Cowper and Shenstone, and Sheridan and Moore, and Shelley and Sir Walter Scott and Burns and Barry Cornwall, and Leigh Hunt and all the famous American poets of the present century. He could also show you the hair of John Milton.

MRS. HARRIET PRESCOTT SPOFFORD, AND
MISS MARY N. PRESCOTT.

THE valley of the Merrimac is one of the most lovely and blessed regions on the earth. It is also one of the best-beloved. No one who was not born beside its magic waters can realize the intensity of affection with which the hearts of its children cling to these broad meadows, rocky clefts, rich intervales, and wooded hills. The sons and daughters of the Merrimac are found through all the wide world, and holding high places in almost every empire; yet the river of their childhood keeps its charm around them, and wins them back, at last, to sleep upon its shores. Like Whittier, in " Revisited," they come joyfully, chanting :

> "Once again, O beautiful river,
>   Hear our greetings, and take our thanks ;
> Hither we come, as Eastern pilgrims
>   Throng to the Jordan's sacred banks."

And no one ever accuses us of extravagant love ; for the charm of our valley falls irresistibly on all who enter its blooming borders.

The famous Brissot, when standing on Pipestave Hill ; the exiled Louis Philippe, riding by the very spot that is our poets' home ; the late Chief Justice Chase, traveling the same road, — numbers of great men, have united in calling the scenery unsurpassed. Bayard Taylor — and who has seen more lands ? — while gazing from Powow Hill, a lofty mount pitched over against the home of Whittier, says that "for quiet beauty it excels anything I have ever seen."

From such surroundings poetry flows as naturally as the river waters, and, while the most luxuriant crop of the Merrimac Valley has been its noble men and women, among them all, its poets have taken a lofty rank. Hannah Gould, Lucy Hooper, and a score of tuneful voices, have made its beauty vocal ; and, to crown them all, most loved and revered, comes the sweet and tender Quaker singer, Whittier.

But not the least of the glories of the Merrimac are the two sisters, of whom I am to tell you, and their home.

On entering the river from the sea, — for our poets' home, like Venice, should be approached by water, — we pass the sandy bar between walls of breakers,

which form the white-lipped river-mouth. Once inside, the stream broadens into a great bay, and the
scene is one of surpassing beauty. On each side the
fragrant salt-marshes stretch far back into the country, "the low, green prairies of the sea," covered with
picturesque hay-cocks, standing on stilts ; while in and
out flow and waver the Black Rock Creek, and Plum
Island River, like winding gleams of light, — and up
the wide stream lies the shining city full in view.

Few sights are more charming than that of Newburyport from the river, when the Eastern sun is glowing in its face. The houses rise back from the shore,
tier beyond tier, until "The Ridge" is crowned with
stately mansions, — and all the whiteness is softened
by that dense foliage which is the joy and pride of the
city.

The tide is on the flood, and sweeps us swiftly along
the narrowing river, past three miles of wharves and
rambling buildings ; past the great ship-yards (what poetry there is in a ship-yard!) ; past little islands with
quaint old houses ;—the shore grows wild and rocky,
hung thick with woods, — when a sudden turn
in the river opens a vision that is like a dream
of fairyland. Set against a background of forest,
hills, and quiet waters, lies a lovely island in mid-
stream. From the left hand of the river swings

a suspension bridge hung high overhead on immense chains; while one, partly covered and wholly picturesque, stretches away to the Salisbury shore. Flanking the island, beyond it, and high in air, the tower of "Hawkswood" peers over the pines, and Laurel Hill lifts up its castellated mansion.

The swift tide is parted by a low point of meadow, where the grass is kept beautifully bright and green by being afloat half the time; and straight back into the heart of the island opens a shadowed glade. God's glory rests on the island: for it is covered with magnificent pines and firs, " an house not made with hands," worthy to be the tabernacle of the Lord. Hiding deep in this loveliness, the quaint roof and broad piazzas of a great brown dwelling throw out their hints of welcome through the trees.

This is Deer Island, the home of Mrs. Harriet Prescott Spofford and Miss Mary N. Prescott. It is the very spot of which Whittier sings :

> "Deer Island's rocks and fir-trees threw
> Their sunset shadows o'er them."

But whether sunset or sunrise, all who pass the island, like "Goodman Macey" and his wife, must come under its delicious shadows; for all around its rocky rim the great pines drop their cones into the river.

Let us hug the bank and, drifting softly up the
stream, use neither oar nor sail, for we must not scar
the burnished face of the waters.   One ripple comes
by us from the point, wavering and musical, but its
form soon dies along the stream, and its spirit seems
to have flown into the pines overhead, where it sings
in whispers — like one lulling a babe into sleep — at
the faintest thought of a far-off breeze.

The water is a magic mirror, for, looking closely at
the reflections, we see through them and beneath
them, — clear depths, cool liquid nooks among
sunken rocks waving their bright green flags in the
rushing tide.

A pebbly beach fringes the cliffs for a little way, —
the pines still shadow it, however ; a rustic seat peeps
out from the brink ; a heavy gloom falls athwart the
river, and the great bridge glides overhead.   Here a
bold rock thrusts its face over the stream, and a great
fir on its brow leans out, almost horizontal, as if, like
Narcissus, it was in love with its shadow, and ready
to plunge into the deep below.

Sloping clefts in the rocks are cushioned thick with
pine needles, and little seats hold out their arms and
certainly say "Come."

In one cleft, near the upper point of the island, we
will moor our boat and land.   Every step now is a

delight.   Under foot are delicate mosses and soft turf, and overhead the white clouds play hide-and-seek through the trees.   The view from this western point falls like the hush of Sabbath evening over the spirit.

No opening is seen in the river, for half a mile beyond it makes a sudden bend to the northward.   On the left bank the perfect beauty of "The Pines," a noble grove, comes down to bathe its feet in the cooling waters; while, farther up stream, "Moulton's Castle," once the home of Sir Edward Thornton, British Minister at Washington, dominates the whole landscape from its lofty perch, and, far beyond, the rolling hills of Amesbury show their serried fields of corn.   Around the foot of the "Castle," too, but out of sight from the island, is the grove of "The Laurels," made famous by Whittier in several of his poems.   On the Salisbury bank of the river, also, the trees come down to the water, but here many oaks are mingled with the pines, and the effect is delightful to the eye.

One gigantic pine stands on the very point, watching the bending river play the tide ripples around its feet.   This is the "Hawkswood" estate, and the tower of the stone chateau lifts its black head over the forest.   It was built by Rev. J. C. Fletcher, the author and lecturer; and here passed many of the

girlhood days of his daughter, Miss Julia Fletcher,
who wrote the recent " Kismet," in the " No Name "
series.

Deer Island is seven acres large,
and we have yet trodden but
one part. We will cross the
highway that cuts it in twain,
and enter the grove on the

DEER ISLAND SUSPENSION BRIDGE.

eastern side. Just across the river is that perfect model of a school for boys, "Eagle Nest," with its pleasant grounds, and down the stream the striped roofs of Eagle Island's arbors shine through the woods.

But the glory of this end of our island lies all about us. It is in the towering pines and firs, every one of which is a joy and a wonder. They are most musical poems, grown from God's love and bounty, — stately and majestic, for they have "fed on honey-dew, and drunk the milk of Paradise." Everywhere we ramble, they outspread their arms over us and murmur "Benedicite." It is almost as if we "heard the voice of the Lord God walking in the garden in the cool of the day;" and surely, they are expecting Him, for, like the throng before the gates of the Holy City, they have cast their garments on the ground for Him to tread upon, and all living things, even the tiny moss-cups at their roots, do cry "Hosanna!"

The pine-needles lie everywhere beneath our feet, and our voices take the hint and fall into a hushed whisper. Some of the trees were born twins, and have never been separated by time or tempest, growing side by side from the same root.

Surely no happier spot can be found under heaven where one could lie to dream, and wake, and then to dream again ; to catch, in his half-unconscious moments of awakening,

> "That old voice of waters, of birds, and of breeze,
> The dip of the wild fowl, the rustling of trees ! "

and then, sliding down the gulfs of sleep, to

> " Hear in his dreams the river's sound
> Of murmuring on its pebbly bound,
> The unforgotten swell and roar
> Of waves on the familiar shore."

These rocks could tell a wondrous story if they would ; and even now, while we drowse, there come the trumpet-notes of Whittier's song :

> " But hark ! from wood and rock flung back,
> What sound comes up the Merrimac ?
> What sea-worn barks are those which throw
> The light spray from each rushing prow ?
> Have they not in the North Sea's blast
> Bowed to the waves the straining mast ?
> Their frozen sails the low, pale sun
> Of Thule's night has shone upon ;
> Flapped by the sea-wind's gusty sweep
> Round icy drifts and headland steep.
> Wild Jutland's wives and Lochlin's daughters
> Have watched them fading o'er the waters,
> Lessening through driving mists and spray,
> Like white-winged sea-birds on their way."

For ages before Columbus sat, a fair-haired boy, on the wharf at Genoa, looking into the blue Mediter-

ranean, and dreaming of new worlds, the fierce
vikings of Norseland are said to have sailed past our
island; and, not far from here, a fragment of a statue
has been found, which some attribute to their hands.

But we want to see the house, although just now we
are hardly conscious of it, we are so " steeped in the
happy summer weather;" and if we stay here long
we shall forget all care, like the " Lotus Eaters," and
feel, with Miss Prescott in her song, that

> " Life is enough, no matter whether
> One be a bird or a flower ! "

The dwelling is one of those grand, old-fashioned
farm-houses, built to last as long as the island, and
when folks had plenty of room and plenty of timber
to put round it. It used to be a tavern, also, and it
actually seems to laugh as we come up to it, with
memories of the jollity it has seen in days gone by.
But there is a different air about it now. It has been
remodeled somewhat, without and within; and, while
there is no lack of laughter around it, it stands with a
quiet and stately grace. There is store of joy there
now, but it is different; as the song that steals out
into the hushed night from the poet's lattice is different from that which makes the rafters ring over the
bowl of cider.

It was hard to pass the piazza before, for surely none ever gave a broader welcome. It actually looks like its master, — generous and genial. We cross over and enter the spacious doorway. Sitting here in the quiet, and looking out on the beauty beyond, it would almost seem nothing strange if three shining ones should appear, as they did to Abram when he sat in the door of his tent on the plains of Mamre.

But we must turn about. What a splendid hall! (I know that is a "woman's word," but nothing else will do.) To me it is the noblest part of the house. The staircase is broad and quaint, and above, it is open clear through the house, giving it an air of spaciousness and grandeur. Below, too, it is wide and cool, a most delicious retreat in the heat of the day, a perfect temple for quiet, unspoken worship in the hush of evening. To the left of the hall is the parlor; and, once within, it is hard to get away, there is so much to feast the eye, and, if I may say it, so much to charm the mind; for here the family sit and make the *home*. Of course you would expect choice books and pictures; and so there are, — one of the latter a sketch from Mrs. Spofford's "Sir Rohan's Ghost," drawn and given by the sister of Mr. Howells; and another, a grand, terrible old painting of the tragic scene in the life of Christ, — a dark piece, which glooms impressively by candlelight. But the glory of the parlor, — which fills the whole breadth of the house and is very spacious — is the fire-place. This is very unique and rich. It is made of the "precious serpentine," a green, veined rock of the loveliest tints, and which takes a very high polish. It was taken from Mr. Spofford's quarry at the "Devil's Basin," in Old Newbury, and it is the first time, I think, that the stone has ever been put to this most appropriate use.

From the rear of the parlor opens the library, and from that Mr. Spofford's office. The library is well stored from floor to ceiling, and very attractive with books, busts and pictures. Just the place for one to sit in, with a book across the knees, and — look out of the window; for a perfect flood of beauty is outside, and it would be a very interesting volume, or a very hard task, that could keep *my* eyes from roaming, in there.

One picture in the library I must speak of, for love of "auld acquaintance." It is an engraving of Horace Vernet's "Le Poste du Désert;" and many a time in my boyhood's days I have stood before it, and forgot all else while I watched the great swing of the camel's feet, and listened to hear their soft fall on the Saharan sands, or gazed into the swart face of the

Bedouin rider. With the rest of the house we have nothing to do, for you know we were not invited to "bed and board."

If we go back into the parlor we shall see the family; and those you are the most interested in are the two poets. Mr. Spofford is himself a poet, and has written strong and graceful verse; but with him it is only the bead upon the wine-cup; his profession forces him to drink at other fountains. You and I would not think them as pleasant — "Blackstone" and "Coke on Littleton;" for he is a lawyer, you know.

There is a brother, too, who is a poet if he would be; I well remember, in our school-boy days, his reading a poem of rare melody and rhythm. You see it is a family of genius. Indeed, it has been a family of marked intellectuality all the way down.

The Prescotts can boast — but never do — of as noble a lineage as any of our good old New England families. Sir William Pepperell, Sir John Brydges, and a host of worthies, were their ancestors. Prescott, the historian, was a cousin; and Mr. Evarts, our Secretary of State, and the famous Hoar brothers, of Massachusetts, are nearer still.

Miss Prescott has very kindly given you her portrait, for which we are much indebted to her; so I only speak of her poetry, after telling you that she is tall and slender, with beautiful corn-silk hair, and quiet, charming ways.

Thousands who regard Mrs. Spofford with love and reverence, and yet can never meet her, long to look upon the semblance of her face. But no entreaties

Miss Mary N. Prescott.

can prevail upon her to "have her picture taken." And truly, no hard-lined photograph can fitly repro- duce the charm of her face, for this lies largely in its ever-varying and sympathetic expression, and, above all, in its deep spirituality. Having once, in- deed, looked into her eyes, you can never forget them.

Have you ever seen the face of Mrs. Browning?
I do not say that Mrs. Spofford looks just like her;
but I do say that I never look on the face of the one
but the face of the other comes instantly before me.
There is a strong resemblance between the cast of
head and features in the two poets; and very much of
that tender, spiritual depth which made Mrs. Browning so beautiful is seen in the face of our own singer.
There is reason for it, indeed; for Mrs. Spofford
has a deep religious nature, making her genius glow
like the coal from off the holy altar, which touched
the lips of the prophet, and led him to glorious song.

Mrs. Spofford has a very light complexion, and is
of medium height, though her delicate and slender
figure makes her seem tall.   Or is it a peculiar charm
of carriage that gives this impression?   For Milton's
verse,

> " Grace was in all her steps,"

may well be applied to her, — whose pace is rapid,
and yet with so little apparent motion that she seems
to glide rather than to walk.

Mrs. Spofford has not written as much for young
folks as her sister, but her stories and poems meant
for you I doubt not you have read over and over
again.   You know she stands at the head of the
" word-painters;" so far, indeed, as to be solitary and

alone. She writes — as your editor says — with the brush. Her work has the glow of a New England autumn; at times it is wild as New England's "September Gale," and then suddenly there will fall upon it the sacred hush of a New England Sabbath.

As specimens of the "word-painting" for which Mrs. Spofford is so justly famous, read that account of the night on the lake, in "Midsummer and May."

"Ever and anon they passed under the lee of some island, and the heavy air grew full of idle night-sweetness; the waning moon, with all its sad and alien power hung low, — dun, malign, and distant, a coppery blotch on the rich darkness of heaven. They floated slowly, still; now and then she dipped a hand into the cool current, — now and then he drew in his oars, and, bending forward, dipped his hand with hers. The stars retreated in a pallid veil that dimmed their beams. Faint lights streamed up the sky, — the dark yet clear and delicious. They paused motionless in the shelter of a steep rock; over them a wild vine hung and swayed its long wreaths in the water, a sweet-brier starred with fragrant sleeping buds climbed and twisted, and tufts of ribbon-grass fell forward and streamed in the indolent ripple; beneath them the lake, lucid as some dark crystal

sheeted with olive transparence a bottom of yellow
sand; here a bream poised on slowly waving fins, as

"The staircase is broad and quaint."

if dreaming of motion, or a perch
flashed its red fire from one hollow
to another. The shadow lifted a degree, the eye
penetrated to farther regions; a bird piped warily,

then freely, a second and then a third answered,
a fourth took up the tale, blue-jay and thrush,
cat-bird and bobolink, — wings began to dart about
them, the world to rustle overhead. Near and far
the dark pines grew instinct with sound, the shores
and heavens blew out gales of melody, the air broke
up in music. He lifted his oars silently; she caught
the sweet-brier, and, lightly shaking it, a rain of dew-
drops dashed with deepest perfume sprinkled them;
they moved on. A thin mist breathed from the lake,
steamed round the boat, and lay like a white coverlet
upon the water; a light wind sprang up and blew it
in long rags and ribbons, lifted and torn, and streaming out of sight. All the air was pearly, the sky
opaline, the water now crisply emblazoned with a dark
and splendid jewelry, — the graved-work of a sapphire; a rosy fleece sailed across their heads, some
furnace glowed in the east behind the trees, long
beams fell resplendently through and lay beside vast
shadows, and giant firs stood black and intense
against a red and risen sun; they trailed with one
oar through a pad of buds, all unaware of change,
stole from the overhanging thickets through a walled
pass, where, on the open lake, the broad silent yellow
light crept from bloom to bloom and awoke them
with a touch. How perfectly they put off sleep! with

what a queenly calm displayed their spotless snow, their priceless gold, and shed abroad their matchless scent!

"He twined his finger round a slippery serpent-stem, turned the crimson underside of the floating pavilion and brought up a waxen wonder from its throne to hang like a star in the black braids on her temple. An hour's harvesting among the nymphs, in this rich atmosphere of another world, and with a loaded boat they returned to shore again."

This is poetry that haunts the memory, like a sweet unknown voice heard in the night, weaving a song familiar and filled with some undying joy of our far-off days.

But I like even better her sea-scenes, and in these she surpasses all women who have ever written. Mrs. Spofford is a genuine product of our New England coast. The east winds have blown her through and through, — not to chill her powers, but to sweep the chords of her heart into a rare, rich melody, — now soft and dying, now wild and crescent — to which the glorious sea itself delights to thunder its bass before her feet. She rides the sea, — that soft, sleek, purring monster, with hidden claws and terrible fangs, — as Una rode the lion. One can almost hear her saying, with Byron,

"The waves bound beneath me as a steed
    That knows his master."

Let us turn to Mrs. Spofford's story of " The South
Breaker," which is one of those breakers that we
passed as we came into the Merrimac on our way to
her island home.

"There was the Cape sparkling miles and miles
across the way, unconcerned that he whose firm foot
had rung last on its flints should ring there no
more ; there was the beautiful town lying large and
warm along the river ; here gay crafts went darting
about like gulls, and there up the channel sped a
large one with all her canvass flashing in the sun, and
shivering a little sprit-sail in the shadow as she went ;
fawning in upon my feet came the foam from the
South Breaker, that still perhaps cradled Faith and
Gabriel. But as I looked, my eye fell, and there
came the sea-scenes again, — other scenes than this,
coves and corners of other coasts, sky-girt regions of
other waters. The air was soft that April day, and I
thought of the summer calms ; and with that rose long
sheets of stillness, far out from any strand, purple
beneath the noon ; fields slipping close in shore, emerald backed and scaled with sunshine ; long sleepy
swells that hid the light in their hollows, and came

creaming along the cliffs. And if upon these broke
suddenly a wild glimpse of some storm careering over
a merciless mid-ocean, of a dear dead face tossing up
on the surge, and snatched back again into the
depths, of mad wastes rushing to tear themselves to
fleece above clear shallows and turbid sandbars, —
they melted and were lost in peaceful glimmers of the
moon on distant flying foam-wreaths, in solemn midnight tides chanting under hushed heavens, in twilight
stretches kissing twilight slopes, in rosy morning
waves flocking up the singing shores. And sitting so,
with my lids still fallen, I heard a quick step on the
beach, and a voice that said 'Georgie!' and I looked,
and a figure, red-shirted, towered beside me, and a
face, brown and bearded and tender, bent above me.

"Oh! it was Dan!"

Much of Mrs. Spofford's work — as much of
Whittier's also — receives thus its local coloring from
the peculiarities of our neighborhood. To all who
know our woods and waters, our quiet or storm-blown
coast, her enthralling pictures carry sweet or terrible
secrets to which other eyes must be dimmed.

The "South Breaker" lies off one end of Plum
Island, and is easily reached with dry feet at low
tide. Only the other night I stood on the farthest

point, and saw the moon burst through the fog-clouds in broken masses of lurid red, melting into one perfect globe as the fog moved on.

But if Mrs. Spofford writes with such terrible vigor of the sea, when she crosses the narrow strip of sand which makes Plum Island she leaves the wildness of the waste of waters behind her, and her voice falls low and musical as the winding river among the sedges. Let us hear her as she sings "Inside Plum Island." It is but half a mile from Plum Island River to the fierce Breaker ; yet how vast a change in the tones of her harp !

> 'We floated in the idle breeze,
>   With all our sails a-shiver ;
> The shining tide came softly through,
>   And filled Plum Island River.
>
> "The shining tide stole softly up
>   Across the wide green splendor,
> Creek swelling creek till all at once
>   The marshes made surrender.
>
> "And clear the flood of silver swung
>   Between the brimming edges,
> And now the depths were dark, and now
>   The boat slid o'er the sedges.
>
> "And here a yellow sand spit foamed
>   Amid the great sea meadows,
> And here the slumberous waters gloomed
>   Lucid in emerald shadows.

. . . .

"Around the sunny distance rose
   A blue and hazy highland,
And winding down our winding way
   The sand hills of Plum Island —

"The windy dunes that hid the sea
   For many a dreary acre,
And muffled all its thundering fall
   Along the wild South Breaker.

. . . .

"Beneath our keel the great sky arched
   Its liquid light and azure;
We swung between two heavens, ensphered
   Within their charmed embrasure.

. . . .

"Broadly the bare brown Hundreds rose,
   The herds their hollows keeping,
And clouds of wings about our mast
   From Swallowbanks were sweeping.

" While evermore the Bluff before
   Grew greenly on our vision,
Lifting beneath its waving boughs
   Its grassy slopes Elysian.

" Here all day long the summer sea
   Creams murmuring up the shingle ;
Here, all day long, the airs of earth
   With airs of heaven mingle.

"Singing we went our happy way,
   Singing old songs, nor noted

Another voice that with us sang,
   As wing and wing we floated,

" Till hushed, we listened, while the air
   With music still was beating,
Voice answering tuneful voice, again
   The words we sang repeating.

" A flight of fluting cchoes, sent
   With elfin carol o'er us —
More sweet than bird-song in the prime
   Rang out the sea-blown chorus.

" Behind those dunes the storms had heaped
   In all fantastic fashion,
Who syllabled our songs in strains
   Remote from human passion ?

" What tones were those that caught our own,
   Filtered through light and distance,
And tossed them gayly to and fro
   With such a sweet insistence ?

   .   .   .   .

" One standing eager in the prow
   Blew out his bugle cheerly,
And far and wide their horns replied
   More silverly and clearly.

" And falling down the falling tide,
   Slow and more slowly going,
Flown far, flown far, flown faint and fine
   We heard their horns still blowing.

   .   .   .   .

" In vain at night we sought the sound —
    Stars over us and under
Through all that watery wilderness
    Building a world of wonder;

   .   .   .   .   .

" In vain our lingering halloo,
    Our roundelay untiring,
No silver cry chimed far or nigh
    Of all that silver choiring.

" O, never since that magic morn
    Those strains the boatman follows,
Or piping from the sandy hills,
    Or bubbling from the hollows.

" Yet long as summer breezes blow
    Waves murmur, rushes quiver,
Those warbling echoes everywhere
    Will haunt Plum Island River ! '

Mrs. Spofford's descriptions are always faithful to
nature. She paints scenes as they are, — then calls
up their souls for us to commune with. That is a
true incident of the echo; on the way to "The Bluff"
this echo was found — never noted before — among
the sand-dunes; but on the return it refused to answer, and has been silent ever since. There is one of
her poems which has always been a favorite of mine
and I want to quote it wholly; because, like well-
woven music, not a tone can be dropped without
breaking the chord. It will show you, too, how she

goes deep down and through the things of sense,
piercing to the spirit and turning the light of her
luminous eyes upon its secrets.   You cannot yet understand the full depth of this poem, but as you grow
older you will all have the experience — no mortal
can escape it :

LISTENING.

" Her white hand flashes on the strings,
   Sweeping a swift and silver chord,
And wild and strong the great harp rings
   Its throng of throbbing notes abroad :
Music and moonlight make a bloom
Throughout the rich and sombre room.

" Oh, sweet the long and shivering swells,
   And sweeter still the lingering flow,
Delicious as remembered bells
   Dying in distance long ago,
When evening winds from heaven were blown,
And the heart yearned for things unknown.

" Across the leafy window-place
   Peace seals the stainless sapphire deep ;
One sentry star on outer space
   His quenchless lamp lifts, half asleep ;
Peace broods where falling waters flow,
Peace where the heavy roses blow.

" And on the windless atmosphere
   Wait all the fragrances of June ;
The summer night is hushed to hear
   The passion of the ancient tune :
Then why those sudden tears that start,
And why this pierced and aching heart ?

> "Ah, listen! We and all our pain
> Are mortal, and divine the song!
> Idly our topmost height we gain, —
> It spurns that height, and far along
> Seeks in the heavens its splendid mark,
> And we fall backward on the dark!"

Her first captivation of the public was romantic enough. When but a school-girl she wrote a story called "In a Cellar," and sent it to *The Atlantic Monthly*. The editor was astonished at the talent displayed and at the perfect familiarity with French society life. He would not believe it possible in one so young. He thought it must be a translation, and returned it to her with that rather aggravating, but very flattering, decision. But good Colonel Higginson, then a clergyman here, wrote to the editor vouching for the genuineness of her work, and it was instantly received.

Her published books are "Sir Rohan's Ghost," 1859, written while yet a girl, but giving great promise; "Amber Gods and Other stories," 1863, in which are found the most wonderful displays of her mastery of color and incident; "Azarian," 1864, and "New England Legends," a collection of tales of the old colony times. Among her writings for children, some of the most charming are "Christmas," a beautiful hymn of the Saviour-babe, in *Our Young Folks* for December, 1865; "The Portrait," a powerful

THE LIBRARY.

sketch in the same periodical for February, 1865 ; and " Arnold and His Violin," in *St. Nicholas* for November.

Miss Prescott's first appearance, too, was when a school-girl ; her mother's quick perception detecting a " composition " that was worthy of a wider hearing — which it quickly got. In reading the charming poems Miss Prescott has given to the world, you see at once that she looks at all things through Nature, as through transparent glass. All her sweet and tender thoughts are set forth through the medium of flowers and books and trees, " Flower-talk," " Praise," " Waiting," are such ; and if she were to teach a school of children it would surely be done in the same way ; as you may see from " Flora's Multiplication," and " Sue's Lessons : "

> " Wait, little one, wait ;
> The crocus comes in its purple gown,
> The marigold soon wears its golden crown,
> And the robin will not be late."

> " Twice one are two,
> Violets white and blue ;
> Twice two are four,
> Sunflowers at the door."

She has a special love for birds, and perhaps it is this that makes her write such sweet songs. She enters into all their joys and sorrows, and seems to understand all their charming ways. You may see

VIEW AT THE WESTERN POINT.

this in such poems as "Out in the Shower;" "Out
in the Storm;" "The Bird's Nest," and "The Bird's
Song." She loves even the plain weeds, and sings, in
"Summer's Invocation:"

> " Come mullein and sorrel and rue,
> Fill the humble niche waiting for you,"

and especially in "In Summer:"

> " While simple weeds seem saying, in grateful transport praying,
> Unto Him our praises all belong! "

Her heart is full of love and faith and trust in God,
not only for herself, but for all her dear friends in
nature.   These feelings well up like clear springs
through beautiful grasses in "Listening," "The
Golden-rod," "Why?" "Winter" and "Springtime." There is rare depth and tenderness in her
verse, too, when dealing with subjects which call it
out. Some years ago a little babe came to Mrs.
Spofford, — a noble-looking boy, with his face full of
"that imperial glory whence he came." I can never
forget that face; but he soon fled back again. A
glimpse of her sister's thought then, can be caught in
"Rest," "Morning-Glory," and "Good-Night, Little
Star;" but one little poem you must let me repeat
entire, because it has always seemed to me the most
perfect thing of its kind in the English language:

"Sound asleep ! no sigh can reach
   Him who dreams the heavenly dream ;
No to-morrow's silver speech
   Wake him with an earthly theme.
Summer's rains relentlessly
   Patter where his head doth lie ;
There the wild fern and the brake
   All their summer leisure take ;
Violets, blinded with the dew,
   Perfume lend to the sad rue —
Till the day breaks, fair and clear
   And no shadow doth appear."

Miss Mary Prescott's only book is "Matt's Folly," but her stories for the young folks, if collected, would make a large and very inviting volume.

One most important member of the family, I must not forget. He was, but is, alas ! no longer ! I mean Hans. Hans was not a Dutchman — he was a Spitz dog. "None knew him but to love him," except the boys who made faces at him in the street. He was not made for boys, but for "family use." And I am tempted to add that other remark of advertisements, "Every family should have one." He was heroic outside the house ; in the parlor gentle and gallant as any carpet-knight. It might be said of him indeed, as of the old Roman : *Suaviter in modo ; for-titer in re.* He was beautiful and wise ; but even such must die. He succumbed to poison a few weeks ago, and his demise left a gap in the family, and an empty place in their hearts. "Do doggies gang to heaven when they dee?" asked the little Scotch boy of his dominie. If you were to ask our poets, they would certainly answer "Yes."

MRS. CELIA THAXTER.

D EAR CHILDREN, would you like me to tell
you a word of one whom you, too, doubtless
have come to count among your own? She that was
the "Spray Sprite" of that enchanting island, with
its wealth of deep-sea life — that point of rock up-
lifted from the sea, and crowned with its jeweled light,
now golden and then red? She who, in later years,
sang the sweet, brave, matchless songs that the great
sea had whispered into her heart?

Upon your maps you will find on the wee bit of
coast of New Hampshire a city called Portsmouth.
It is an old, old town, with a great harbor, and ship-
ping, and a navy yard; and it is the birthplace of
Celia Thaxter. It is a quaint, interesting old town.
Down by a small pier of its own is a staunch little
steamer, called Appledore. If you step on board of
it, you will soon be steaming out on the still waters of

this fair, wide harbor. To the right and left are fine views — wharves, boats, points of land, orchards, old forts, and other picturesque objects, through which the boat winds its way. After you have gone thus two or three miles, you find the land on either hand receding from you, and that you are really out at sea.

If the breeze is at all stiff, then the stout little steamer, with its flying banners and gay people, is tossed about on the great, green, white-capped waves as if it were of very small account. It would make you laugh to see it, yet you wouldn't be a bit afraid. Somehow you would trust this funny, stout-hearted, determined little boat, that despite the waves seems to know its own mind and make decided headway.

By and by several queer little gray moles appear through the haze on the horizon. You approach. They grow larger, yet scarcely above the level of the sea. If it is evening, you see the constant twinkle of the red and golden light. Presently you draw near to one of the islands — for such they are — with its gray rocks lifted against the sea, and the lights glimmering from the one great house. With music, and waving flags, and merry bustle, the boat steams proudly up to the wharf, and here you are at Appledore.

You go to sleep that night with the sea singing in

your ears. Next morning you are wakened — how do you suppose ? By a bugle horn ! Its notes wind over the rocks, and waters, and slumbering place,

"Ah, so loud, and wild, and sweet !"

that you open your eyes, believing life to be some dear, joyous, restful and magical thing. Where are you ? In an Alpine glade ? Or in the deep forests of the Scottish Highlands ? Nay ; rather, away out your window is the limitless sea. It plashes upon the rocks forever. You forget there are such things as great cities, with their toiling multitudes. You forget the clattering mechanism of the world. The millions of households dotted over the land, the schools, the books, all seem so far, far away. You forget all but these little gray rocks in the ocean, with their own peculiar life, until it seems as if you had fallen upon that fabled lotus-land, where those who once go remember their own country no more.

And this is Appledore, the largest of the Isles of Shoals, with its mile or more of rocks, chasms and cliffs, adorned with short abundant herbage, with its pleasant house for the entertainment of those attracted thither, with its grassy slope to the wharf, where a fleet of small boats are in waiting to convey one, at will, to the adjacent islands, or whithersoever you would go.

APPLEDORE ISLAND.

"The cottage where every summer Celia Thaxter holds her little court."

To the right of the great house, and higher up, quite among the rocks, is the cottage where, every summer, Celia Thaxter holds her little court.

The cottage, which is a detached portion of the hotel, is as plain a house as ever you saw. No bay-windows, balconies, or other pretty appendages; no fanciful gables, or Gothic points; no newness of paint; no vines or trees. Only a plain, two-storied house, with its dormer-windowed attic. A homely house built on the rock, and perched in severe relief against the sky.

Across the front, and at one side, is a piazza shaded by canvas awnings. Here, from one of its swinging hammocks, or from the parlor windows, one can look over a peacefully animated scene: the great house, and grassy slope, with knots of people here and there; the small harbor, the neighboring islands, and the white sails dotting the vast water.

At the front of the cottage is a small yard, enclosed by a picket fence. It is full of flowers. I do not mean prim and decorous beds, and flowers staying where they are put, within their well-clipped borders. But a yard *full* of flowers — full to the fence-top and covering every inch of ground with their glad luxuriance. Not a weed anywhere — quite crowded out by these burning, glowing, starry, gladsome creatures.

Somehow, by reason of the soil and air, all flowers here have a freedom of growth and brilliancy of hue not elsewhere found, — an intense loveliness!

In this yard nasturtions, pansies, marigolds, sweet-pease, mignonette, and other homely flowers, live out their very best life. It is a pleasure to see something live at its very best — gladly, generously, and un-dwarfed!

Indeed, you cannot step anywhere there is a bit of soil all over this island, without crushing some sweet-faced eye-bright, pimpernel, or other interesting flower. No wonder Mrs. Thaxter's poems are full of them. Nor is it strange her little parlor is adorned with them! They, too, like the sea, have whispered into her heart their dear and subtle meanings.

> "The barren island dreams in flowers, while blow
>   The south winds, drawing haze o'er sea and land;
> Yet the great heart of ocean, throbbing slow,
>   Makes the frail blossoms vibrate where they stand."

Wild morning-glories twine about her chandelier, and bud and bloom every day, nourished by some hidden glass of water. A pearly shell, pendent be-low, is always full of the "barbaric splendor" of nasturtion bloom. Single marigolds have their hon-ored place. There are oblong cups full of pansy-faces, looking up into your own. Flowers, flowers everywhere in this little parlor !

A globe of water by the window holds a star-fish, a sea-urchin, or other strange creatures that the same tender hand has gathered from their secret haunts.

In one corner of the room is the writing-desk, where now and then, in leisure moments, those unique, rapid notes are dashed off to numberless friends far away. Bright, virile little notes, as clear and compact as the intellect that indites them. In the corner opposite is an upright piano.

Curious story-telling sketches and drawings adorn the walls. Over the mantel, at one time, was a sketch of herself, laying drift-wood upon the fire. At the time Harry Fenn drew this sketch, the parlor was severely simple, and charming in that simplicity. It is much changed since then. Now it is filled with harmonious color, and numerous added objects of interest. Yet, happily, it retains its original character. Were this lost, it would be a grief to its many friends. A recent movement to refit the entire cottage met with a protest from those to whom this parlor had become endeared, and it was left undisturbed for the present.

Underneath the mantel is the grate itself, on which, at evening, the drift-wood is piled. In the light of

its cheery flame, countless wise and witty people
have, one time or another, been made glad.

They listen, perhaps, to some thrilling tale of
wreck or disaster, or ghostly tradition, or back and
forth is tossed a sparkling fire of wit, and quaint or
funny anecdote. The most engaging humor it is that
touches the heart, or makes so merry, that peals of
many-voiced laughter drift out the door and windows
into the mysterious twilight, where the sea sighs and
the flowers are nodding in the wind.

Or, may be, there is music from the piano, or some
wonderful melody from the violin; or there is a
song. Perhaps it is one of Mrs. Thaxter's own
songs, for many or them have been set to music.
Maybe " Farewell," " Foreboding," " We sail toward
evening's lonely star," or this one of exceeding
sweetness :

> ' Sing, little bird, O sing !
> How sweet thy voice, and clear,
> How fine the airy measures ring
> The sad old world to cheer !

> " Bloom, little flower, O bloom !
> Thou makest glad the day ;
> A scented torch, thou dost illume
> The darkness of the way.

> " Dance, little child, O dance !
> While sweet the small birds sing,

THE DRIFT-WOOD FIRE.

And flowers bloom fair, and every glance
    Of sunshine tells of spring.

" O bloom, and sing, and smile,
    Child, bird, and flower, and make
The sad, old world forget awhile
    Its sorrow for your sake."

A few miles south from Appledore is the light-house, fixed upon its rock, White Island. This was the childhood home of Celia Thaxter. Hither she came when she was but four years old, sailing across the sea to this lonely rock with her father, mother, and brothers, and all the household gods.

This little girl, Celia Leighton, with her two brothers, led a life quite unlike that of other children. They lived very simply and secluded — rarely seeing other than their own people at any season; while in winter they were provisioned like a garrison, and lived isolated, with the cheery light above, and the tempestuous sea about them. She knew nothing of schools, nor of the vast machinery of inland life. She had no child books. Shakespeare, it is said, was the lightest reading within her reach. Fancy yourselves, dear young people, without your school-companions, your child papers and magazines, your games and puzzles.

But do not think this was a demure and lonesome

little girl. Far from it. She had indeed, her child-
life. She possessed a young and glad spirit, that all
the years since have not been able to filch away.

The great sea was her beloved companion. She
passionately loved the sky, and clouds, and stars, and
the sun that made glory in the east and west, the
changing moon, the streaming northern lights — the
very winds seemed human things, that laughed or
played with, that chided or caressed her. The waves
that whitened the sea, and that broke madly on the
bleached rocks, filled her with delight. The thunder,
the lightning, and the rain ; every bird that floated
over, whether sandpiper, gull, the sparrow or the
loon — every sail that glided across, thrilled her with
glad interest. Ah! this was a brave, fearless, and
joyous little girl.

> "Under the light-house no sweet-brier grew,
>   Dry was the grass, and no daisies
> Waved in the wind, and the flowers were few
>   That lifted their delicate faces.
>
> "But, O, she was happy, and careless, and blest,
>   Full of the song-sparrow's spirit ;
> Grateful for life, for the least and the best
>   Of the blessings that mortals inherit."

That wee bit of rock in mid-ocean was no prison to
her, but a most dear and wonderful home. Every

inch of it was most precious. There were shells, white, and gray, and gold-colored, and violet. Myriads of many-colored creatures and plants inhabited the still pools. Much tenderness she felt for these, wondrous and beautiful as they are, that dwelt, each in its own peculiar fashion, among the rocks. Their wisdom was more amusing than the best game ever played. Then there was always something new appearing — if but the coming and going of the tide, or the drift-wood washed ashore from some sad wreck or far-off coast.

Here, too, a few flowers and grasses grew. There was one root of fern that she watched and cherished year after year. She gathered the golden-rod, and crowned herself with garlands of wild pink morning-glories, or with a crown of the marigolds that grew on her wee plat of ground; and the gold-colored shells were strung into necklaces like beads. So adorned, and lithe and graceful as a fawn, she flitted from rock to rock, the sprite of an enchanted island.

The picture is before us in this song : —

THE SANDPIPER.

" Across the narrow beach we flit,
  One little Sandpiper and I ;
And fast I gather, bit by bit,
  The scattered drift-wood, bleached **and dry.**

The wild waves reach their hands for it,
   The wild wind raves, the tide runs high,
As up and down the beach we flit —
   One little Sandpiper and I.

" Above our heads the sullen clouds
   Scud black and swift across the sky ;
Like silent ghosts, in misty shrouds,
   Stand out the white light-houses high.
Almost as far as eye can reach,
   I see the close-reefed vessels fly,
As fast, we flit along the beach —
   One little Sandpiper and I.

" I watch him as he skims along,
   Uttering his sweet and mournful cry ;
He start not at my fitful song,
   Or flash of fluttering drapery.
He has no thought of any wrong ;
   He scans me with a fearless eye ;
Staunch friends are we, well-tried and strong,
   The little Sandpiper and I.

" Comrade, where wilt thou be to-night,
   When the loosed storm breaks furiously ?
My drift-wood fire will burn so bright !
   To what warm shelter canst thou fly ?
I do not fear for thee, though wroth
   The tempest rushes through the sky ;
For are we not God's children both,
   Thou, little Sandpiper and I ? "

But the chief of her pleasures was sometimes at
evening to light the lamps in the light-house tower.

It was so great a thing for a little maiden to light the stately ships upon their way!

This strong, lightsome nature loved her freedom well. Wide nature, with its beauty, was far more dear to her than either dolls or "patchwork." Perhaps she disliked small, irksome duties even more than do other children.

Afterward, when she was spirited away to the mainland to live, she found everybody so busy it was astonishing to witness — doing all sorts of work under the sun. She that had studied the great out-of-door world so eagerly, now as closely considered this "patchwork" of our every-day living. Slowly, very slowly, she found out a secret worth all the beauty she had lost. Let me tell you it in her own words to the children : —

" I'll whisper it in your ear. This is it : That work is among the best blessings God gave the world ; that to be useful and helpful, even in the smallest ways, brings a better bliss than all the delightful things you can think of put together, and this bliss is within the reach of every human being."

I assure you, young WIDE AWAKES, one thing is true. She who was the Spray Sprite is able to furnish your Cooking Club with the best and surest receipts they ever found.

And is not good thinking as valuable in the homely as in the fine affairs of life? I think so.

One summer day, not long ago, Mrs. Thaxter took a few friends across the water from Appledore to her childhood home.

There was still the dangerous landing where the little maid once delighted to wait at evening, with a lamp, to light some loved one into the unsafe cove. There were the white-bleached rocks, among which, long ago, the little dun cow caught her hoof, and so came to her death, much to the grief of this same little maid. There, best of all, was the stone cottage. "This," she said, "is the window where my flowers grew in winter." A deep, roomy window it was. Here, doubtless, did the child witness the awful "wreck of the Pocahontas," which you will find among her poems.

Up from the cottage the near-covered way led to the tower, whitewashed within, and an opening or two looking out upon the sea.

The tower itself at the base was large enough to hold the winter's stores, that were always provided with as much forethought as if the island were a ship fitting out for an arctic voyage. Everything *is* entirely "ship-shape" in and about the light-house.

Up the winding stairway the party ascended to the

very top, where the light is flashed out over the sea.
If you look into the lenses of the lamp, the views
reflected are the prettiest pictures you ever saw.   You
look out the windows, and the views themselves are
wonderful, so far above you are, and the sea on every
side at your feet.   The vast extent of water nowhere
broken save by the islands, a fishing-smack, and here
and there a sail, —

> " As idle as a painted ship
> Upon a painted ocean."

Once more below, they climb about the cliffs, watch
the breakers wash the barnacle-covered rocks ; then,
just as the sun is seemingly dipping into the waves of
the radiant west, the party, laden with wild morning-
glory vines, re-embark for home.

Nearing Appledore, the rudder gets entangled in a
cable that forms a part of the moorings for the small
fleet anchored off the rocky shore.   The amateur
oarsman must row — who is to manage the unshipped
rudder?   The poet-captain, with a few dexterous
movements of her masterly hands, makes all right
again, and they merrily go their way.

And " how does she look ? " you ask ?   Ah, that is
a hard question, and words are very poor things to
paint with.

First, think of all the fretfulness, complainings, dis-content, selfishness, narrowness, and ugliness you ever saw in faces — then know that this lady of whom I write has a face as far from these as freedom is from bondage.

And do you not know how pleasant it is to look into a bright room full of pictures, and books, and flowers, and color, and all sorts of lovely furnishings, quaint and surprising? — with a constant fire upon the hearth that sparkles, gleams, and glows, and illumines the whole?

Just so it is to look into this face. It is one to inspire you with the belief that this is a glad and glorious world. It is a face also that draws a lovable child to itself. This you would know, had I not told you, from this —

SLUMBER SONG.

" Thou, little child, with tender, clinging arms,
    Drop thy sweet head, my darling, down, and rest
Upon my shoulder, — rest, with all thy charms;
    Be soothed and comforted, be loved and blest.

" Against thy silken, honey-colored hair
    I lean a loving cheek, a mute caress;
Close, close I gather thee, and kiss thy fair
    White eyelids, sleep so softly doth oppress.

" Dear little head, that lies in calm content
    Within the gracious hollow that God made
In every human shoulder, where He meant
    Some tired head for comfort should be laid.

" Most like a heavy folded rose thou art,
    In summer air reposing, warm and still ;
" Dream thy sweet dreams upon my quiet heart,
    I watch thy slumbers, naught shall do thee ill."

Her head is exquisite ; it has the proud grace that
queens in our childish dreams possess. This you
might have thought from the poem " Courage."
About it the dark-brown hair, so early mingled with
gray, is snugly arranged, usually in encircling braids.
Her eyes are deep blue, and her cheeks are slightly
bronzed in summer with the strong sea-breeze. Her
figure is tall, full, lithe, and of exceeding grace. So
true an artist is she, that, whether she will or not,
whatever she touches, however homely, is lovely in
the doing, and beautiful when done.

Dear children, now we have found the spring
among the rocks, you would like to know why it is
so rich and unfailing? You, too, would know the
secret of this poet's power?

I think it comes from a sweet and powerful soul,
one that would be sorry to see the least little creature
in God's world suffer ; yet one so dauntless that, I

truly believe, were the veriest tempest of sorrow in this sorrowing world to sweep across her, this brave cheer would rise above it as steadfast, and helpful, and clear, as that light in mid-ocean that burns and glows always — now golden and then red.

EDMUND CLARENCE STEDMAN.

THERE appeared in the columns of the *New York Tribune*, in 1859, two poems which attracted a great deal of attention. The subjects were as different from each other as possible, and no one would have thought that the verse in which they were embodied could have come from the same hand. I will tell you about them in a few words. There was at the time, in New York, a Cuban planter, who was said to be very rich, and who was engaged to a young lady in that city. He had purchased for her, as a bridal present, a number of most expensive jewels, which the newspapers of the day described extensively, not forgetting, of course, to mention their cost in dollars and cents. If I remember rightly, they also described the young lady's bridal outfit, silks, laces, and so on, and the sums which they, too, cost. Briefly, then, the newspapers made a public fuss over

what should have been a private matter. It seemed
to a young gentleman who was working in a subordi-
nate position on the *Tribune* that this was a fit subject for a piece of satirical verse, and he accordingly
set to work and wrote one which he entitled "The
Diamond Wedding." It made a great sensation and
a great row; for the father of the young lady, who
saw no impropriety in the notoriety which the report-
ers had heaped upon her in prose, saw a dreadful
impropriety in any reference to her wedding in poetry.
I think, myself, that he should have been grateful to
the poet for not mentioning her name, and the name
of her intended husband; but he thought otherwise,
and sent a challenge to the poor poet. I forget exactly how it was settled, but there was no duel, and
no apology on the part of the poet. Such is the
history of "The Diamond Wedding," which proved
that a new poet had come, and one who could, if he
chose, snatch the laurels from the brows of all the
humorous poets of America. The other poem that I
have referred to displayed a grim kind of humor
which was new in American poetry. It was about a
stern old man who made this year a memorable one
in the history of the United States, by boldly marching with a few men into Virginia, and capturing
Harper's Ferry. "How Old Brown took Harper's

Ferry" made a great sensation, and ought to have
made it, for there was no American poet who might
not have been proud to have written it.

My good friend Bayard Taylor and I were living
together in the same house when these poems appeared, and I remember his coming home one afternoon and telling me that he had that day, or the day
before, met their author in the editorial rooms of
the *Tribune,* and had had a talk with him, and that
he liked him very much. A few evenings afterwards
this likable young poet came to see me, and I was
charmed with him. He had read much, I discovered,
he talked well ; and he was what most poets are not
— modest. His personal appearance you see in the
accompanying portrait; for, though some eighteen
years have passed since then, I see no change in him.
If I could only say the same of myself!

Such was my first meeting with Edmund Clarence
Stedman. I asked him to show me his poems
printed and unprinted, for he told me that he had
enough to make a small volume, and he did so. I
read them with great care ; I corrected them where I
thought they needed it, and I tried to get a publisher
for him. I think that my opinion was not without
weight with the gentleman who became his publisher,
— the late Mr. Charles Scribner. "Poems, Lyrical

and Idyllic," which was issued in the spring of 1860, was and is the best first book that I ever read. The two poems that opened it showed that the writer had read the greatest poet of our time, Alfred Tennyson ; but they also showed that his own originality had not been overpowered by his admiration for this master. "Penelope," the second poem, was and is worthy to be read with Tennyson's noble poem of "Ulysses." The hand of a fine Greek scholar is visible in every line. That he was familiar with the scenery of New England, and the early life of its people, was evident in "The Freshet," which is still the best example of American idyllic poetry. We feel in reading it that Mr. Stedman knew what he was writing about.

He is a born New Englander, a native of the land of wooden nutmegs, Connecticut. He comes of a good family, and a poetic family. One of his ancestors, the Rev. Aaron Cleveland, wrote poetry, I am told, though I have never seen any of it, and a cousin, the Rev. Arthur Cleveland Coxe, is well known as a writer of religious verse. He may be said, indeed, to have inherited poetry from his mother, who figured in Dr. Griswold's "Female Poets," and later as the author of a tragedy called "Bianco Caprello."

Mr. Stedman was born in Hartford on the 8th of

Edmund Clarence Stedman

October, 1833. When he was about two years old he
was sent to Norwich, where he lived with his great-
uncle, Mr. James Stedman, by whom he was strictly
trained. At any rate it was the fashion, forty or fifty
years ago, in New England, to train young people
strictly, and a good fashion it was, too, for some of
them. Whether it was the best training for a poet
may be doubted.

Uncle Stedman, who was a jurist and a scholar,
looked after the education of his brilliant nephew,
who was thoroughly grounded in his native tongue.
At the early age of sixteen he was sent to Yale College, where he was among the foremost in English
composition and Greek. He wrote an English poem
for a periodical which was published by the students,
and a very clever poem it was considered. The discipline of Yale was stricter than suited the mercurial
temperament of the young poet; he fell under the
censure of the college authorities, and quitted college
without taking a degree. His error, whatever it was,
could not have been a very grave one, for the Univer-
sity afterwards enrolled him among the alumni for
1853, with the degree of Master of Arts.

When he was nineteen he was managing a newspaper at Norwich. In the following year he married
a Connecticut girl, and became the owner of *The*

Winsted Herald, which soon rose to be one of the most important of the political papers in the State, and the most influential literary paper ever published in a country town. Of the life of Mr. Stedman during the next five or six years I know nothing, except that the latter part of it was spent in New York. Whether it was ambition which sent him there, or the desire of bettering his fortune, he has never told me, but I imagine it was both.

I have no doubt but that he had to struggle to obtain a foothold in literature, — every unknown man of letters has to struggle in a great city, — but he obtained it, for when I first knew him he was writing on *The Tribune,* as I have already said.

Mr. Stedman was living among the Bohemians, five score or otherwise, when I first visited him, and with him were his wife and his children, two boys the youngest of whom, Master Arthur Stedman, is now fitting himself to go to Yale College, where I hope he will take any degree that he wants, even that of the Grand Panjandrum, if they confer it there.

Mr. Stedman remained on *The Tribune* until *The World* was started, when he transferred his talent to that journal. This was in the fall or winter of 1860. He was one of the editors of *The World* when Fort Sumter was fired upon, and when the news of the firing was sent over the wires he wrote a poem upon it, which was one of the first, if not the very first, poem of any note which the impending war awoke. When the war broke out he went to Washington as the army correspondent of *The World*, and a very able one he proved himself. I forget whether his letters excelled those of other correspondents for accuracy, but they certainly excelled them in spirit.

He was at the first battle of Bull Run, where the North was routed, as we all remember. Other correspondents sent letters to their papers about it, but none came from him. "Where is he?" his friends asked, but nobody knew.

Two, or perhaps three, days passed before he returned to New York. The next day there appeared in *The World* a long and graphic letter about the lost battle which he had witnessed, — a letter which was the town's talk for days. Altogether it was the best single letter written during the whole war.

Towards the close of the war Mr. Stedman resigned his position on "*The World*, and entered the office of Attorney General Bates at Washington. In January, 1864, he returned to New York with his family, and published his second collection of verse, "Alice of Monmouth," which may be described as a little poetical novel. The opening scenes are laid in Monmouth Co., New Jersey ; the middle and later ones in the battle-fields and hospitals of Virginia. We are introduced to Hendrick Van Ghelt, a wealthy old farmer of Monmouth; then we pass to his son Hermann, a cold, calculating man of the law ; at last we come to his grandson Hugh, a noble, manly youth, in whom the smouldering embers of the Van Ghelts survive, kindling a flame as royal as it is high.

Hugh falls in love with Alice Dale, whom he sees for the first time in the strawberry fields. He marries her, and, being disowned by his father, the young couple settle in an old farm-house which Hugh's grandfather had given him years before.

The rebellion breaks out, and Hugh is off for the wars with a company of horsemen, as their captain. The quiet house-life of the young wife, and the stirring field-life of the young soldier, are placed in contrast, the latter leading to a picturesque description of an encampment, and a spirited cavalry song, which is supposed to be sung by the brave troopers of the North.

Then we have a glimpse of a military hospital in Washington, with Alice therein as a nurse ; and there is a description of the cavalry fight in which Colonel Hugh Van Ghelt is wounded, and from which he is borne away to die in a country hospital, with his wife and repentant grandfather by his side.

Such is the story of "Alice of Monmouth."

Here is the cavalry song I have just spoken of:

"Our good steeds snuff the evening air,
    Our pulses with their purpose tingle;
The foeman's fires are twinkling there;
    He leaps to hear our sabres jingle!
            HALT!
    Each carbine sent its whizzing ball:
    Now, cling! clang! forward all,
            Into the fight!

"Dash on beneath the smoking dome;
    Thro' level lightnings gallop nearer!
One look to heaven! No thoughts of home!
    The guerdons that we bear are dearer.
            CHARGE!
    Cling, clang! forward all!
    Heaven help those whose horses fall:
            Cut left and right!

They flee before our fierce attack!
    They fall! they spread in broken surges!
Now, comrades, bring our wounded back,
    And leave the foeman to his dirges.
            WHEEL!
    The bugles sound the swift recall:
    Cling! clang! backward all!
            Home, and good-night!"

There is a notion about, and many people entertain it without thinking, that a man cannot be at one and the same time a poet and a man of business. It

is a mistake. Fitz Greene Halleck was for many
years a competent clerk of John Jacob Astor.
Charles Sprague was for forty-five years teller and
cashier in a Boston bank. Samuel Rogers, the English poet, was all his life a banker, and a very successful one, too. To these names must be added that of
Edmund Clarence Stedman, who put himself at the
head of a firm of stock-brokers, which he started
shortly after his return to New York. They had a
suite of offices in Exchange Place, and dealt in government securities, railway stocks and bonds, and I
know not what besides, including petroleum, in which
fortunes were then being made and lost with great
rapidity.

I saw less of Mr. Stedman now than before, for he
had his business to attend to and I had mine. I knew
nothing of longs and shorts, puts and calls, and he
knew nothing of exports and debentures, and other
custom-house matters.

Mr. Stedman, the stock-broker, was still Mr. Stedman the poet, as the readers of our magazines occasionally saw. Five years passed before he made
another collection of his verse, which appeared in
1869, under the title of "The Blameless Prince, and
other Poems." I shall not tell you the story of
"The Blameless Prince" — you have already guessed

that it is a story poem, — nor anything about it except that I think it grew, in some mysterious way, out of a book that Queen Victoria had written about her dead husband, — " Life in the Highlands," I think it was called.

Mr. Stedman looked the subject over with me before he wrote it, and I — but I must not tell tales out of school. So much, or rather so little, concerning " The Blameless Prince." There are twenty-seven miscellaneous poems in the volume in which it appeared. Among others is a poem about " Country Sleighing," which no other American poet could have written, and which I have always thought the best sleighing-song in the language. Another, entitled " Laura, My Darling," is a poem addressed to his wife. Here is a stanza from it:

> " Laura, my darling, there's hazel-eyed Fred,
> Asleep in his own tiny cot, by the bed;
> And little King Arthur, whose curls have the art
> Of sending their tendrils so close round my heart;
> Yet fairer than either, and dearer than both,
> Is the true one who gave me in girlhood her troth;
> For we, when we mated for evil and good,
> What were we, darling, but babes in the wood?"

It is a charming glimpse of the home-life of a young poet, is it not, this little picture of Mr. Sted-

man's wife and children ?   Equally charming, but **not**
as true, is this pretty song, for while there is a Frederick Stedman and an Arthur Stedman, there is **no**
Katherine Stedman and no Elizabeth Stedman that
I ever saw or heard of.

"WHAT THE WINDS BRING.

"'Which is the Wind that brings the cold?'
   The North Wind, Freddy; and all the snow;
And the sheep will scamper into the fold
   When the North begins to blow.

"'Which is the Wind that brings the heat?
   The South Wind, Katy; and corn will grow,
And peaches redden for you to eat,
   When the South begins to blow.

"'Which is the Wind that brings the rain?'
   The East Wind, Arty; and farmers know
That cows come shivering up the lane
   When the East begins to blow.

"'Which is the Wind that brings the flowers?'
   The West Wind, Bessy; and soft and low
The birdies sing in the summer hours,
   When the West begins to blow."

Four years after the publication of "The Blameless Prince," Mr. Stedman brought out the first collected edition of his Poetical Works. In 1875 he
published his "Victorian Poets," a collection of essays

on a number of English singers who have illustrated the reign of Queen Victoria.

I have mentioned one mistaken notion that many people entertain, namely, that a man cannot be a poet and a man of business ; but I have not mentioned another, namely, that a poet cannot be a critic. If poets are not the best critics of poetry, musicians are not the best critics of music, architects of architecture, and painters of painting. The idea is absurd !

Mr. Stedman's " Victorian Poets " is the most important contribution ever made by an American writer to the critical literature of the English poets. It is not a book to be read, however, by the young readers of WIDE AWAKE ; but it is a book which they ought to read when they come to the last of their teens. Mr. Stedman is living in New York, and is still in business as a stock-broker.

If any reader of this brief paper has any money to invest in stocks, I dare say that he will invest it for him. What money *I* have I generally invest with the butcher, the baker, the candle-stick maker, and other prosaic men of business, and not with my poetical friend, Edmund Clarence Stedman.

THOMAS BAILEY ALDRICH.

"AS we drove through the quiet old town, I thought Rivermouth the prettiest place in the world; and I think so still. The streets are long and wide, shaded by gigantic American elms, whose drooping branches, interlacing here and there, span the avenues with arches graceful enough to be the handiwork of fairies. Many of the houses have small flower gardens in front, gay in the season with china-asters, and are substantially built, with massive chimney-stacks and protruding eaves. A beautiful river goes rippling by the town, and, after turning and twisting among a lot of tiny islands, empties itself into the sea. The harbor is so fine that the largest ships can sail directly up to the wharves and drop anchor. Only they don't. Few ships come to Rivermouth now. Commerce drifted into other ports. The phantom fleet sailed off one day, and never

came back again. The crazy old warehouses are
empty: and barnacles and eelgrass cling to the piles
of the crumbling wharves, where the sunshine lies
lovingly, bringing out the faint spicy odor that
haunts the place, — the ghost of the old dead West
India trade!"

It is thus that Mr. Aldrich, in his clever book entitled "The Story of a Bad Boy," truthfully charac-
terizes that once famous old town by the sea, which,
on the maps at least, goes by the name of Portsmouth.
He has omitted to say, however, that the quaint old
city is peopled with the shadowy shapes of many generations, and that, like all old towns in New England,
it has its queer people, its romantic and eccentric traditions, and that antique flavor of aristocratic better
days, in comparison with which the snug briskness of
a modern town seems cheap and mean. Around lie
woody hills and emerald meadows, through which the
broad river goes brimming to the sea. At the decaying wharves, now and then, rest the sea-worn hulks,
thither drift the song and story, tradition and adven-
ture, terror and romance, of the men who "plough the
raging main."

It was in this very same town, which he pictures so
well, that Mr. Aldrich was born, on the eleventh of
November, 1836; but, before he "had a chance to be-

come very well acquainted with that pretty New England town," 'his parents removed to New Orleans, where the first few years of his life were passed, and where, also, he developed some very queer notions with regard to Northern people in general and Yankees in particular. "To be frank," he says, in the book already quoted, "my idea of the north was about as accurate as that entertained by the well-educated Englishmen of the present day concerning America. I suppose, the inhabitants were divided into two classes, — Indians and white people ; that the Indians occasionally dashed down on New York, and scalped any woman or child (giving the preference to children) whom they caught lingering in the outskirts after nightfall ; that the white men were either hunters or schoolmasters, and that it was winter pretty much all the year round. The prevailing style of architecture I took to be log cabins."

With these singular ideas developed in his mind, and, in truth, "a Northern man with Southern principles," young Aldrich returned to Portsmouth to be educated. The sea voyage was comparatively pleasant, and the boy became wonderfully attracted by an old weather-beaten tar, whose head was quite smooth and flat, as if somebody had sat down on him when he was very young, but which, nevertheless, was stored with a rich fund of anecdote and good humor.

The account of all this, and of his arrival in Boston harbor, of the ride to Portsmouth, and of his school-life there, is given in that almost inimitable of books, "The Story of a Bad Boy." This story is about as nearly autobiographical as the author dared to make it; and, therefore, whoever wishes to know more of Mr. Aldrich's early years than can possibly be told in this chapter, should of course take occasion to read this book, that is, if he has not done so already.

During his stay in Portsmouth, Aldrich dwelt under the roof of his grandfather, "a hale, cheery old gentleman, as straight and as bald as an arrow," whose domestic affairs, however, were under the immediate charge of a maiden sister, a very philanthropic personage, whose strongest weak point was a belief in the efficacy of "hot drops" as a cure for all known diseases. The boy fared admirably in the company of his elders, and, albeit he had some peculiar whims of his own, he was allowed to do pretty much as he pleased, — except on Sundays, which were, indeed, most dreadful days to him!

And no wonder, for nothing was done to make these days seem cheerful. Gloom began on Saturday evening and ceased late on Sabbath night, and, during the hours of its continuance, genial converse, harmless books, smiles, lightsome hearts, all were banished. The Sabbath-school hour was the pleasantest through the day, for young Aldrich liked the Sabbath-school where all was sunshine and everybody had a bright face. The meeting, which followed, was a return to the gloom, as witness this assertion : —

"I go to meeting, joining my grandfather, who doesn't appear to be any relation to me this day. Our minister holds out very little hope to any of us of being saved. Convinced that I am a lost creature, in common with the human family, I return home behind my guardian at a snail's pace. We have a cold dinner. I saw it laid out yesterday. There is a long interval between this repast and the second service, and a still longer interval between the beginning and the end of that service. After meeting, my grandfather and I talk a walk. We visit — appropriately enough,—a neighboring graveyard. I am by this time in a condition of mind to become a willing inmate of the place. The usual evening prayer meeting is postponed for some reason. At half past eight I go to bed."

Of such a direful character were most of the Portsmouth Sabbaths, — dreaded not only by young Aldrich but by every other boy as well, who chanced

some thirty odd years ago, to be a dweller in a New
England village. Sunday is a blessed day, and
therefore it shouldn't be made a day freighted with
awful gloom and terror ; and surely when, if not on
the Lord's day, ought young and old hearts to be
cheerful, hopeful, and full of life and spirit?

Shortly after his arrival at Portsmouth, Aldrich
was put to school, — at the Temple Grammar School
at the farther end of the town. A Mr. Grimshaw
kept here, " a quiet, kind-hearted gentleman. Though
a rigid disciplinarian, he had a keen sense of justice,
was a reader of character, and the boys respected
him." It was not long before the new comer fell into
the ways and notions of his fellows. As he himself
admits, these latter took a great deal of nonsense out
of him, and forced him to become more manly and
self-reliant. In New Orleans, he had labored under
the delusion that the world was created exclusively
on his account: at Portsmouth, he discovered that it
was not!

But, as I have already said, I cannot repeat the
story of those school-days, though, for us, the interest
attached to them exceeds that of any other period of
life. You will find the history of them, written by
one of the principal actors, in the book already
alluded to ; and, if I were to write it over again, it is

to be feared that I should only write in the very same words.

It is well that you should know that young Aldrich was a diligent and faithful student; that, although

THOMAS BAILEY ALDRICH.

fond of sport and an adept in mischief, — of which, by the by, there was always much going on, much to the annoyance of the sober and more sanctified citizens of the place, — he was yet fond of books, and rarely

deserved or received the reprobation of his instruct-
ors. It is pleasant, after these many years that
have lapsed between boyhood and the present, to
know that the teacher, of whom mention was made
above, still lives, and to me has addressed these
words :

"With the hundreds of pupils who have been under
my instruction, there is *not one* for whom I entertain a
higher regard and a purer affection than for Thomas
Bailey Aldrich."

Golden words are these, and I know that they are
earnest and full of heart. And, reader, is it not one
of the pleasantest thoughts imaginable, the knowledge that, perchance, we may be so lovingly remembered by him who taught us in early life, and whom
we have supposed gone to dust long years ago?
Such a tribute is more than gold to a man who merits
it.

Mr. Aldrich was in his fifteenth year when his
father died, and the circumstances governing his
future life were thereby materially altered. All along,
he had been hoping to go to Harvard College, to
complete the course of education already begun ; but
now both the dream and the hope vanished.

One day, when he was not yet over his disappoint-
ment, a letter came from an uncle in New York,

offering him a place in his counting-room. He accepted the proposal, although it was hard for him to
give up becoming a Harvard man.

But why, it might be asked, was his uncle so urgent
in pushing him into a business life? "The cause was
this," — says the historian of these years, — "he was
afraid that I would turn out to be a poet before he
could make a merchant of me. His fears were based
upon the fact that I had published in the Rivermouth
Barnacle some verses addressed in a familiar manner
'To the Moon.' Now, the idea of a boy, with his
living to get, placing himself in communication with
the Moon, struck the mercantile mind as monstrous.
It was not only a bad investment, it was lunacy."

With the close of his school-days at Rivermouth,
the "Story of a Bad Boy" — not such a very bad
boy, either, as one might suppose, — also ends. Like
a fantasy the past rolls back, and the future begins;
the limit betwixt boyhood and manhood is soon over-
stepped, and now it is, in the roaring, tearing, and
enterprising metropolis, the great New York, that the
poet first sees life as it is, instead of as he would
have it.

For three years he remained at his desk in the
counting-room. He worked faithfully enough at his
task, but each day the task grew more and more dis-

tasteful, and poetry had indeed more charm for him than all the figures in the world.

Occasionally, he took advantage of some leisure moments to weave verses after his own way ; and thus it happened that a very good poem now and then saw the light and set most readers to thinking. "Baby Bell" — one of the most popular poems in our literature, — was written by Mr. Aldrich while he was yet in his nineteenth year.

When the announcement of the authorship was made no one was willing to believe that a mere boy could have written so *fatherly* a poem, — for did not the verses betoken a most intimate knowledge of the mysteries of infant life ? Such was the fact, however, and such it must remain.

"Baby Bell" has always been very generally admired by all classes of readers, and deservedly so, I think, for it contains some of the most delicate and sweetest touches in the language. What, for instance, can be more tender and pathetic than the following : —

> "At last he came, the messenger,
>   The messenger from unseen lands.
> And what did dainty Baby Bell ?
>   She only crossed her little hands,
> She only looked more meek and fair !
> We parted back her silken hair,

We wove the roses round her brow,
    White buds, the summer's drifted snow, —
Wrapt her from head to foot in flowers,
    And thus went dainty Baby Bell
Out of this world of ours ! "

When the three years were up, the poet forsook a business life and chose to follow instead a purely literary existence. He believed that that was his proper field of usefulness, and that there were ways enough open to yield gain to the worker.

At first, he secured a situation as " reader" for a large publishing house in New York ; and as manuscripts were pretty plentiful in those days, and his literary judgments were usually quite sound, he derived considerable pecuniary advantage from the new employment.

Reading the works of others, however, did not consume the whole of his time, and, as occasion offered and the spirit moved, he wrote original articles on every conceivable subject, — poems, essays, stories, sketches, and whatever else was prompted. While many of these productions were of an ephemeral character, and scarcely worthy of remembrance now-a-days, a few pieces are still cherished and preserved in the printed works of the author.

In these years also, Mr. Aldrich was editorially connected with the *New York Evening Mirror*, the

MR. ALDRICH'S HOUSE AT PONKAPOG.

Home Journal and the *Saturday Press;* and at the same time furnished articles for *Putnam's Magazine*, the *Knickerbocker*, *Harper's Monthly*, the *Atlantic Monthly*, etc., etc.

In 1854 he published his first book of poems, calling it "The Bells;" and, two years later, was printed "*Daisy's Necklace*, and what came of it" — a work now out of print. In 1858, appeared "Baby Bell, and other Poems," and "The Course of True Love;" in 1861, "Pampina, and other Poems," and in 1865, Messrs. Ticknor & Fields' edition of his poems, in the blue and gold series.

In 1866, this publishing house, having perfected the plan of an eclectic weekly journal, called *Every Saturday*, Mr. Aldrich was invited to come to Boston to take charge of it. Everybody, — or at least most of our older readers, — knows with what admirable ability and success this publication was conducted. In 1874, the favorite weekly was merged into another periodical of a similiar character, and Mr. Aldrich retired from journalism. He still continued his connection with the *Atlantic Monthly*, in which, indeed, almost all of his genuine successes have been made, among them, "Margorie Daw," "Prudence Palfrey," and other short and interesting stories.

I have omitted to state that Mr. Aldrich was

married to a New York lady in November, 1865, and came immediately to Boston. It was to this young couple that another poet, Bayard Taylor, addressed the following exquisite sonnet:

A WEDDING SONNET.

TO L. W. AND T. B. A.

Sad Autumn, drop thy weedy crown forlorn,
　Put off thy cloak of cloud, thy scarf of mist,
　And dress in gauzy gold and amethyst
A day benign, of sunniest influence born,
As may befit a Poet's marriage-morn!
　Give buds another dream, another tryst
　To loving hearts, and print on lips unkissed
Bethrothal kisses, laughing Spring to scorn!
　Yet, if unfriendly thou, with sullen skies,
Bleak voices, or moaning winds, dost menace wrong,
　Here thou art foiled ; a bridal sun shall rise,
And bridal emblems unto these belong:
　Round her the sunshine of her beauty lies,
And breathes round him the springtime of his song.

In 1875, Mr. Aldrich and his wife, in company with a party of friends, made an extensive tour abroad, visiting the principal cities and also many of the out of the way places in England, Ireland, Scotland, France, Germany, Italy, Hungary, Austria, Bohemia, etc. He was away from home somewhat more than six months, traveling almost constantly. A rapid survey of the ground passed over by the party is given in an article, entitled "From Ponkapog to

Pesth," published in the *Atlantic Monthly* for January, 1877.

Of course it goes almost without my saying it, that Mr. Aldrich's foreign experiences have furnished him with the *motifs* for several of his later poems, notably those found in the volume "Flower and Thorn," printed in the present year. This volume, together with the one entitled "Cloth of Gold, and other Poems," contains all the poems on which the author places any value or cares to have remembered. The last half of "The Queen of Sheba" — the author's latest fiction — also deals largely with Switzerland, and involves some very careful studies of that picturesque land.

Mr. Aldrich has several times been honored by republication abroad. A complete collection of his prose writings is published at Leipzig ; and his stories have been translated and republished in Paris. It is hardly necessary for me to add that such honor is richly deserved, for no writer in American literature can write more vigorous and clearer prose, draw such delicate *genre* pictures, and weave more pleasing and fanciful conceits. His poetry, altogether too choice, it would seem, to win the admiration of a multitude, has in it an oriental depth of color and airiness for the few who can appreciate the truly poetic.

In respect to personal appearance, Mr. Aldrich is somewhat above the medium height, of slender yet vigorous form, and possesses a pale, brown complexion and gently wrought features. A stranger would easily, and perhaps rightly, judge him to be a man of the world; for, while his experience of life has been most varied, neither care nor trouble has left an impress upon his forehead, or stolen from his age the freshness and buoyancy which so right belong to youth.

He is to-day "Tom Bailey" still, and as ready to share with any one in having a jolly good time.

Mr. Aldrich's home, properly speaking, is in Boston, where he owns a residence at the West End. For the present, however, and chiefly on account of the health of his two boys, — twins of eight years of age, — he lives at Ponkapog, a part of the town of Canton, in Massachusetts. Although a very charming place, Ponkapog was never noted for its enterprise and the location of a railroad some two or three miles distant has left it very much in the condition of Bailey's Four Corners, described by Mr. Aldrich in his story of "Miss Mehetable's Son."

The house, as is shown by the illustration, is an old fashioned, two story house, built at the beginning of the present century, and is partially screened from

THE STUDY.

the road by cherry trees and by a hedge of arbor vitæ, presided over by two ancient and shiftless-looking buttonwoods.

Back of the house, the grounds fall away gently to a stream and an old mill-pond, on which stands a deserted and decaying mill, which was utilized during the late war for the weaving of soldiers' cardigans. Along the margin of the stream which, after wandering all round the grounds, finds its way out on the Neponset meadows, and so to the ocean, great quantities of water-cresses, ferns and curious wild flowers grow, the early cowslip and the pitcher plant among them.

Mr. Aldrich's library — of which, unfortunately, we cannot give the reader a glimpse, as the room was in a process of renovation at the time of our visit — contains a large number of volumes admirably selected and adapted for the work of a literary man. In the "study" — shown in the engraving — an air of perfect refinement and taste reigns, — the large, open fire-place reminds one of the good old times, and when the logs are piled high and the flames crackling, one is forced to think it the true home of a poet.

But not always is he at work with his pen, as you might rashly suppose. At the foot of Blue Hill, on the southeast of the town, there is a large pond, well stocked with fish of the choicer sorts. Mr. Aldrich is aware of this fact; and you may be pretty sure that, when not at home, he and the boys are off with hook and line, or perhaps with a shot gun, in search of game. He likes this sort of exercise, and takes a great deal of it in the course of his suburban life.

If I were to speak my mind, I should say that these inclinations are what keeps him in perfect health, happiness and prosperity, — and what more could be wished for?

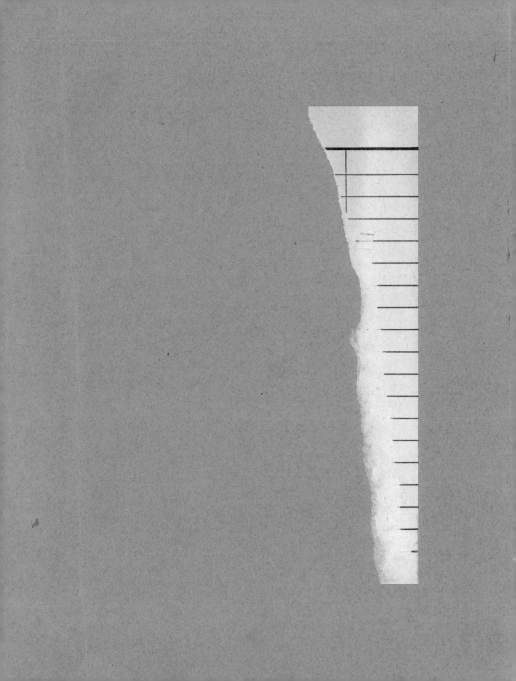